Praise for *A Head Full of*

This is an important book! It is challenging and reassuring at the same time, and combines principles and practice to telling effect. Di-Finizio provides a compelling narrative that is rooted in successful leadership practice and in deep reflection. His focus on ethos is particularly valuable in supporting, as it does very well, a holistic approach that integrates strategies and principles and informs the day-to-day routines and the most important strategic challenges. The book is therefore a powerful model of leadership learning and development and a resource to inform and influence learning across the school.

John West-Burnham, Visiting Professor in Education, University of Suffolk

I have read many leadership books but none get 'down and dirty' with the reality of being a school leader day in, day out. And none give as much space to the importance of what it means to be an adolescent, and the implications of that for school leadership, as this book does. Armando offers sound, practical advice that new leaders (and indeed established leaders) can implement in their own context. Although I would advise reading the book from cover to cover, you can also home in on specific sections that have particular relevance to you. The book is easy to navigate, and the 'What to take from this chapter' crib sheets provide useful summaries.

Hilary Street, education leadership consultant,
writer and former editor of the NAHT Leadership Paper Series

A Head Full of Ethos holds fast to what really matters in schools and sets out clearly how to achieve it. Armando shares his experience in a way that will be helpful to anyone who wants to run their school on truly educational principles. Full of common sense, wisdom and healthy suggestions, and with young people and their futures at its heart, this is the book to keep within reach for constant reference.

Mick Waters, Professor of Education, University of Wolverhampton

Armando has always believed that the best solutions are the simple ones, and this outlook is evident throughout the book. *A Head Full of Ethos* is not just for senior leaders but also for those heading up their first team or even those considering a career in teaching. Current educational challenges are complex and demanding, but this book illustrates that success can be achieved when there is a clear vision and leaders take time to build relationships and listen.

Jacky Kennedy, Chief Executive Officer, Mater Christi Multi-Academy Trust

A Head Full of Ethos complements the many 'toolkits' of school leadership that already exist by encouraging the reader to consider what kind of school ethos they hope to build. Armando argues that by developing a consistent set of values and principles across the school, this will help school leaders to prioritise decisions and make better and more complementary day-to-day decisions for their staff, pupils and wider community. He demonstrates that a clear vision and set of guiding principles is necessary to successfully navigate the wide array of policies, tools and interventions available to contemporary educationalists.

Professor Chris Taylor, Academic Director,
Cardiff University Social Science Research Park (SPARK)

This is one of the most powerful and readable leadership books I've seen in a long time. It should be on every NPQH reading list in the country, and is a must-read for all new and aspiring head teachers. It offers something unique in the field: a guide to making a real difference as a school leader, by someone who has recent, lived experience of turning around and leading some of the most challenged schools in the country. Armando's writing is a real breath of fresh air to read: concise, honest, engaging, and skilfully combining ethos and driving values with practical advice from someone who really knows what they are talking about!

Pippa Whittaker, SEND specialist

In Armando's sinuous reflection on his three decades of experience in leadership, he re-examines his approaches that help shape a school's ethos. Each chapter is packed with insightful and entertaining anecdotes and reflective questions which give the SLT member, head of department and emerging leader ample opportunity to reflect. *A Head Full of Ethos* discerns the individuality of every school and its vision and is punctuated by supporting literature and influential sources yet acknowledges the limitations of following research blindly without considering one's context. Ultimately, it is an energetic and valuable perspective that sheds light on leadership, fostering ethos and direction in a team, maintaining positive relationships and creating a sense of belonging in the community.

Georgina Saunders, teacher of English

A Head Full of Ethos is different to other education publications. It is highly accessible, hugely relevant, an easy read and a compelling experience for any teacher, subject leader, pastoral leader, senior leader or head teacher, all of whom would find it a useful guidebook to explore the many experiences which can happen at any time in any school. As well as addressing the routine activities which impact on the lives of school leaders, most critically it focuses on the lives of those they lead. Written with a focus on the core principles which underpin the practices of school leaders and teachers, its style and presentation leads us to reflect on our own practices, values, principles and the experiences which have moulded these.

Sue Hollister, education consultant and former head teacher

A Head Full of Ethos

A holistic guide to developing and
sustaining a positive school culture

Armando Di-Finizio

Crown House Publishing Limited
www.crownhouse.co.uk

First published by
Crown House Publishing Limited
Crown Buildings, Bancyfelin, Carmarthen, Wales, SA33 5ND, UK
www.crownhouse.co.uk

and

Crown House Publishing Company LLC
PO Box 2223, Williston, VT 05495, USA
www.crownhousepublishing.com

First published 2022.

Image page 117 © elenvd – stock.adobe.com.

Quotes from Ofsted and Department for Education documents used in this publication have been approved under an Open Government Licence. Please see: http://www.nationalarchives.gov.uk/doc/open-government-licence/version/3/.

British Library Cataloguing-in-Publication Data

A catalogue entry for this book is available from the British Library.

Print ISBN 978-178583587-2
Mobi ISBN 978-178583605-3
ePub ISBN 978-178583606-0
ePDF ISBN 978-178583607-7

LCCN 2021949266

Printed and bound in the UK by
Charlesworth Press, Wakefield, West Yorkshire

To Sandra Lane: my wife, friend and mentor.

I am very fortunate.

Preface

As the title would suggest, this is a book about ethos – or, more specifically, school ethos. That feeling you have concerning the nature or soul of a school when you first walk into the building; it has been with me throughout my career, from teacher to head teacher. The further I have progressed into school leadership, the more conscious I have become of how influential school leaders at all levels are in setting the tone for their school and, in turn, defining its general state of health and effectiveness. In other words, it is one of the countless books covering the ins and outs of school leadership. If you have picked it up, I imagine you will have some questions that will require an answer before you invest valuable time and money on it. Here are three questions that I would be asking if I were in your position.

What makes you qualified to write a book like this?

The answer to this is fairly straightforward. I have been a teacher (at the time of writing) for 34 years in seven schools, almost half of this time as a head teacher. Apart from my first school, which was a high-achieving school in a London suburb, the rest have all been in challenging city schools in areas of high deprivation. My first (and only) deputy head position was in a low-performing school which was closed and reopened as one of the first city academies in England. The school saw a year-on-year improvement in results while I was there and was given a good Ofsted rating with outstanding features in two inspections.

Since then, I have had the genuine privilege of leading three different schools as head teacher/principal. The first two in England (Bristol Brunel Academy and Hans Price Academy) were both in the bottom 10 schools in the country with regard to GCSE outcomes and were among the highest excluding schools. They were both forced to close due to poor Ofsted reports and reopen as academies. The third and present school (Eastern High) is situated in Cardiff. It was in a similar position to the other two schools: it was in the bottom three for all deprivation measures across Wales, had extremely high exclusion rates and was ranked among the lowest (if not the lowest) schools for GCSE attainment across the UK. It also failed its inspection to the extent that it was threatened with closure.

The success in my first headship – which had resulted in constantly improving results (we were one of the most improved schools in the country in respect of GCSE grades), a good Ofsted inspection and zero fixed-term exclusions – led to me being asked twice more to apply to lead schools in similar situations. Each time, the outcomes have been similar and all three schools have sustained the systems and practices which made them successful. Each school has also become oversubscribed.

What made you write this book?

When I set out on my career path, I never imagined that I would be the head of three different schools, let alone have successful outcomes in each of them. I will be honest, I have lived most of my life harbouring well-hidden self-doubt and fear of failure. However, I have steadily gained confidence through the good fortune of working with some amazing role models and I have been supported by individuals who have inspired me. This has led me to always aspire to have similar qualities, such as sound moral judgement, articulacy, creativity and leadership. I was also brought up to work hard and never give up. Over the years, this work ethic, along with unrelenting self-reflection, has pushed me to a position where I can confidently acknowledge my accomplishments in each of these three schools.

What made me realise this were the questions I was beginning to be asked, such as what my formula was for turning around a school or how I generated community belief in the school. Many people have also asked whether I have recorded what I have done or planned to write about my experiences. These questions have helped me to begin to take stock of what my colleagues and I have achieved in each of the schools I have led. It is now time that I shared what has worked for us – but it comes with a warning, as described below.

What will I learn that I may not find in other books on school leadership?

Before beginning to work in the teaching profession, each of us has journeyed through our own form of schooling. As we travelled along our career paths, our own action research projects unfolded and developed on a daily basis. Most of us did this unconsciously. However, when we stop and consider all the golden nuggets of experience we have picked up along the way, we begin to realise the extent to which they form a wealth of valuable information. In addition, when we reflect, as I do in this book, on earlier insecurities and errors, we gather additional insights that we may not have noticed as we progressed. All of this together forms our own unique school improvement story, which should be shared in our collective quest to provide outstanding schooling and education for all young people.

In short, this book contains my own unique story, which will explore the elements of school improvement that have worked for me and, just as importantly, examine why some things went wrong. I will also outline the principles that have supported me in developing new ideas, as well as selecting and adapting the ideas of others, in my own schools. I cannot ignore the experiences and findings of others whose work I have drawn on and who have helped me along the way; there is much of value out there.

However, there is a health warning here too, which is that it is all too easy to be swept away by the slew of books that appear on a daily basis, as well as the slew of ideas that flow from social media, telling us how to educate young people effectively. All too often, when an aspect of school ethos or curriculum break down, especially for those in challenging circumstances, the leadership of a school will jump from one idea or initiative to another with little thought as to how it aligns with the school's values and principles. This pick 'n' mix approach can lead to blurred vision and possible confusion. Leaders then wonder why things aren't as effective as they ought to be, and are likely to dive back into the vast knowledge base they have at their fingertips for yet more (and hopefully better) ideas.

Don't get me wrong: books, blogs, pamphlets, journals and articles are our toolbox and the wealth of information they contain provides us with amazing ideas and tried-and-tested examples. However, by becoming over-reliant on the ideas and research of others, we become blind to the big picture in our own school. These ideas increasingly become used as a crutch to support us rather than the means to help us develop sustainable practices organically. The tools we deploy should align with the first principles (explained in Chapter 2) that underpin the school vision and should be used consistently and appropriately in the right place, at the right time and by the right people.

I would like to say that I have always gone back to the first principles of school improvement ever since I first stepped into a leadership role, but sadly this is not the case. My journey has been long and my thoughts have evolved gradually. Now, in the latter part of my career, I feel in a position to articulate my own thoughts and ideas to help others formulate their own practice. This book will give you the means and confidence to take more ownership of what you do, regardless of the position you hold in a school, and hopefully save you much time by helping you to identify what is right for your school or area of responsibility.

To put it another way: don't pick up this book if you are looking for definitive answers. Although there are lots of useful tips and practices which could be used in any school, try not to get too distracted by them and instead aim to identify the consistent set of principles from which they arise.

Although this book encompasses what I believe are the essential ingredients to setting the scene for good teaching and learning, what it does *not* do is tell the reader how to go into a classroom and deliver an excellent lesson. If this were a book about cars, it would tell you how to look after your car, perhaps plan a service schedule and repair it when it breaks down. It might also describe what you might expect in terms of performance and explain the different instruments that make it go. What it would not do is tell you what fuel to use or how to drive it.

Where I have developed ideas that I have read about or seen in other schools, I have tried to acknowledge those that have ignited my thoughts and sent me hurtling down particular paths. Apologies if I have missed anyone out; the zeitgeist really does exist and sometimes I just don't know what sparked a particular idea.

Acknowledgements

I would like to say a big thank you to all those who have helped me along the way.

Some of the leaders who have forced, cajoled and inspired me to become a better leader and person: David Wragg, who first employed me as a teacher and taught me how to stay relaxed in a challenging environment; Warren Wilkinson, my first head of department who helped me to be myself; Steve Foot, my second head of department who taught me never to argue with young people; Vernon King, the deputy who gave me my first leadership role and pushed me to pursue an MA; Patrice Canavan, a head teacher who taught me the difference between leadership and management; Ray Priest, the head teacher who taught me to care; and Sir David Carter, the chief executive who gave me my first headship and developed my confidence as a leader.

Some professionals I have worked with who have just simply inspired me: Jacky Kennedy, a teacher from my early years who showed me how to make teaching fun; Chris Mackintosh, for being a genius whenever I needed one; Brigid Allen and Peter Scholey, the dynamic duo who were always there for me during my first headship and beyond; Pippa Whittaker, for always reminding me to think about *every* child; Graham Powell and Guy Claxton, who opened my eyes to the good habits of learning; Peter Barnard, for showing me what passion really means when it comes to getting it right for young people; and John Corrigan, who injected Zen into my career and taught me to understand myself and others better.

All the staff in the three schools I have led – Bristol Brunel Academy, Hans Price Academy and Eastern High – for their unbelievable patience, hard work and dedication and also for making my time in each of these schools so enjoyable.

The team at Crown House and especially the editors, Daniel and Emma, who, unknowingly, taught me so much.

There are countless others, including the students I have taught. Hopefully I will bump into you again one day and thank you face to face.

With very special thanks to:

Hilary Street, a consultant and friend who has guided me through all of my leadership years. Without her, I would have made a thousand monumental mistakes along the way and certainly not be in any position to write this book.

Sandra Lane, my wife, friend and mentor, who has contributed more to my career and this book than was ever intended when she signed along the dotted line many years ago. Her help with Chapter 3 was especially invaluable and her patience along the way (book and career) has never faltered.

Cyril Payne, a youth worker/behaviour support officer who passed away shortly before publication of this book. Cyril joined me on my first day at Eastern High and was a major contributor to creating the ethos we have today. He dedicated almost all of his working life and social time to improving the life chances of young people and will be sadly missed by many.

Contents

Introduction

Mae ethos ysgol yn addysg ynddo'i hun!

While working as a head teacher in Wales, I was searching for the perfect statement to go on the wall for all to see as they entered our school. I wanted the statement to relate to our school ethos, but nothing felt right until a chance discussion with another head led to him suggesting the Welsh saying above.[1] It translates into English as, 'A school ethos is an education in itself.' Immediately, I knew that this was the statement I had to have, and so I proceeded, without any negotiation or consultation, to have it printed in its Welsh form and up it went on the wall without further ado.[2]

Ethos (the Latin word for character) is, for me, the spirit and driving force behind every good school. It is the manifestation of a school's vision and its underpinning principles. It should enable every student who passes through the school to grow and develop before going on, hopefully, to flourish in life – providing the ethos is a positive one that encourages development and growth. The principles supporting the ethos of a school cannot be ignored, and it is on this premise that I set about writing this book on leadership and school improvement.

Whether you are an early career teacher or an experienced head, on completion of your first walk around a school you will have felt its ethos. During this walk, you may have picked up hints about the nature of the school. Some of these will have been unconscious: perhaps the way the receptionist greeted you when you first entered the building, the relaxed way the staff spoke to the students or the congenial atmosphere at lesson changeover. Other aspects of the school ethos will have hit you directly: the wall displays of students' work, the posters or signs with messages (such as the one I placed at the entrance to our school), the photographs of students taking part in sport or performances, and the school vision displayed in prominent places. In short, when we consider the ethos of a school, there are

---

1   Thank you Edward Jones, the head of Pencoed School (at the time of writing).
2   The reason for having it printed in Welsh was to encourage people to ask what it meant (if they didn't understand Welsh); consequently, it has inspired much thought and discussion.

countless constituent parts and interactions which work together to form the school's character and spirit.

A Head Full of Ethos examines the first steps towards creating a sustainable school ethos which will become the bedrock on which a school inspires its students to flourish and its staff to grow professionally. Although it is primarily a book about headship, it is not just for head teachers. Every member of staff in a school has been appointed to help improve the outcomes for the students – and a positive and consistent school ethos is central to this. For example, if you are a head of department (or aspiring to be one), the same principles that we apply to school development can also be applied to creating a positive and productive ethos in your department.

This requires a deep understanding of the relationship between the school's vision, its underpinning principles, and how this translates into the strategic direction and day-to-day operations of the school. This deep understanding will, in turn, assist you in identifying aspects of the school that are not working so well. It will either give you the tools to deal with these impediments, which are consistent with the principles by which the school abides, or it will provide your head teacher and senior leadership team (SLT) with important feedback about the running of the school. Multi-academy trust (MAT) executives can't lead multiple schools in isolation and neither can school leadership teams; they both need the support of every member of staff.

We all have a responsibility to be critical when necessary, but in order to do this we must be in possession of, and have a full understanding of, the guiding values and principles that sustain the school vision and its systems, processes and practices. The vision, values and principles upheld by the school are the roots of its ethos; these then germinate to form its systems, processes and practices. If head teachers set out to develop the ethos of a school, or if teachers and heads of department try to contribute to the school ethos, they must bear in mind the following: the ethos of a school and the values and principles underpinning its vision are, or certainly should be, congruent with each other. In other words, working in harmony and never coming into conflict. This is one of the reasons why the subsections of this book are described as cogs (more on this below).

Congruence requires clear leadership, which we will explore in more detail in Chapters 1 and 2, but for now it is enough to say that the consistent application of a school's principles will help to form a strong, positive school ethos, leading directly to improved outcomes for the school and its students. Conversely, if there is no clear and consistent ethos, the school will feel disjointed (especially if core principles conflict with one another) and it will become an unhappy working environment for staff and students. Ultimately, this will be detrimental to school improvement and student attainment. At worst, it can cause a school to dramatically fall apart as, sadly, I have witnessed in the past.

For me, happiness is a wide-ranging and vital component of outstanding, flourishing schools. For the school community as a whole, it can range from the degree of congeniality and positive working relationships that exist (as we will explore in Chapters 3 and 4) to the purpose and aims of the school – that is, its nature (Chapter 2). For the individual, it can mean the level of security (in respect of physical safety or job security), individual esteem and aspiration.

This book will focus on how a school can move from being unhappy and directionless to becoming a school that has direction and purpose and is mostly happy. I certainly won't fool myself, or you, that schools can be entirely happy all of the time. However, there is no reason why it is not possible to maintain a consistent direction and purpose.

Reflecting on my three headships, I have come to realise that in each school I have focused primarily on four aspects of ethos. Each of these form a chapter in this book: insightful leadership (Chapter 1); vision, purpose and direction (Chapter 2); care and positive relationships (Chapter 3); and belonging and inclusiveness (Chapter 4). Yes, I have worked hard to develop the quality of teaching and learning in the classroom, but these foundations of ethos are where real and lasting change can happen in a whole school and to all the students. Without these four focal points, fantastic teaching and learning may exist in the school but the children are hostages to fortune. They are dependent on the attributes of their teachers, and not everyone will be guaranteed the same quality of experience in all facets of their school life.

A Head Full of Ethos will look at each of these four areas in turn. There is no particular right or wrong place to start because much of what I consider in this book developed concurrently. However, what each of the four topics have in common is that they all return to first principles. Consequently, this book attempts to answer the following questions:

● What are the basic principles of leadership, regardless of which model you select?

- What are the axioms or uncontested maxims of schooling that every school vision and its underpinning principles should contain?

- What do you need to know about the basics of making, maintaining and managing good relationships?

- What are the key components that make a school inclusive and create a sense of belonging?

Understanding or reacquainting yourself with these fundamental principles will empower you as a leader or a teacher.

This book also asks you to reflect on what you believe in and how you conduct yourself. It focuses on the conscious, strategic and planned practices that reflect our ethos – for example, developing the vision, purpose and direction of the school and the way this comes together through leadership at all levels. The book also encourages you to focus on the day-to-day way you comport yourself at school and the level of care, inclusiveness and positive relationships which contribute towards a sense of belonging and which, in turn, bring the whole school community together.

It is not neat. There are crossovers here but nothing in education is neat; one of the reasons I have chosen to call my subsections 'cogs' is to reflect the holistic and interconnected nature of schools.[3] It is important that you keep this concept to the forefront of your mind as you progress through the book. It is also the reason why I have subtitled this book 'a holistic guide to developing and sustaining a positive school culture'. Everything connects, so we must ensure that the cogs operating in schools really do work together and don't cause abrasion or bring about a grinding halt to progress. Rather than there being a number of vaguely related but discrete tasks with conflicting values and contradictory accompanying behaviours, a successful school ethos – with all its myriad systems and practices – should incorporate the same consistent values and principles throughout. They are the oil that keeps the cogs turning.

---

3   I borrow the concept of cogs from Michael Fullan, who uses them in his comprehensive framework for classroom and school improvement: Michael Fullan, Barrie Bennett and Carol Rolheiser-Bennett, 'Linking Classroom and School Improvement', *Educational Leadership* (May 1990): 13–19 at 15. Available at: http:// www.ascd.org/ASCD/pdf/journals/ed_lead/el_199005_fullan.pdf. Thank you to Richard Jones, currently the head teacher of Ysgol Calon Cymru, who read an early chapter and pointed me in the direction of the cog concept.

Before we progress further, there are a few additional points to bear in mind:

- When I refer to young people, I sometimes call them students, children or young people. The reason I use these different terms – and not just 'student' – is because, at times, I want to emphasise the fact that we are working with children or teenagers. Overusing the term 'student' or 'pupil' can lead to us unconsciously forgetting that these are emotionally charged and not yet fully formed individuals. They are – for want of a better way of explaining myself – different creatures to adults, and if there is one golden rule for teachers then it is never to forget this. Why refer to young people as students and not pupils? There is no real reason other than this is the term I have been most used to using in England, where children tend to be referred to as pupils in primary schools and students in secondary schools.

- I refer to schools as schools (rather than academies) and head teachers as heads (rather than principals) for no other reason than to ensure consistency.

- I am a secondary school teacher and so all of the examples in this book are from a secondary perspective. However, the principles discussed are also relevant to primary settings.

- I have only ever taught in schools in challenging circumstances, and so many of the examples I use are from these schools. Nonetheless, the principles and practices underlying most of what I explore in this book are equally applicable and relevant to any school.

Chapter 1

An Ethos of Insightful Leadership at All Levels

The leadership of a school sets the bar for ethos and keeps us on track when we stray off course. Conversely, leadership can also bring about a systematic breakdown and cause a school to lose all sense of direction, leading to a loss of confidence and respect from the community it serves.

It is the head who primarily sets the scene for a school, and although they require a team behind them to create a great school, nevertheless, they can single-handedly cause it to fail. This also applies to leaders at any level: a head of department can inflict similar damage on their department and a teacher can quickly lose a productive working ethos in their classroom. In short, whether you are a school leader or a teacher just starting out, it is vital that you understand the nuances of leadership.

This chapter covers three areas which experience has led me to believe are at the core of all good leadership:

1   How you perceive yourself and how others perceive you.

2   Self-organisation, clarity and focus.

3   Understanding leadership and how this influences the way you work and relate to your colleagues.

To explore leadership fully and what it entails, we will unpick these three areas in the following ways:

● We begin in Cogs 1.1–1.3 by investigating the self: who you are, how people perceive you and how you model the behaviours you hope to see reflected across your school or department. Exploring these cogs will better equip you to answer the following questions:

   › How do I perceive myself as a leader?

   › How do others perceive me as a leader?

> How well do I model the behaviours I want to see?

● In Cogs 1.4 and 1.5, we look at how to organise yourself as a leader, focusing on how you ensure clarity in your intentions, building a team around you and getting the most from them, and how to remain focused and systematic when it comes to school improvement and caring for your staff and students. These cogs will enable you to answer the following questions:

> How can I pace myself and others to ensure we do things well?

> How do I manage the expectations of others, especially those who hold us to account?

> How do I prioritise effectively and avoid the 'noise'?

● Finally, in Cogs 1.6–1.8, we explore the essence of leadership and working with people: how leadership differs to management, different models of leadership, building and leading a team and getting the most from those you lead. It is as much about understanding others – knowing their strengths and being sensitive to their needs – as it is about simply managing them. These cogs will help you to answer the following questions:

> To what extent am I a leader compared to being a manager?

> What attributes should I look for in my team? Do they complement my own?

> How do I enable others to grow through effective delegation?

Cog 1.1: Sort out your ego!

I had four pressing worries as I walked tentatively towards the entrance of the school on my first day as a head teacher:

1   *I wanted to make a lasting impression,* describe my hopes and aims clearly and, hopefully, inspire the majority. I thought of all the heads I had worked

under and their first presentations to staff, either as a new head or at the beginning of the year; so many of them were inspirational. Would I create that same lasting impression?

2   I thought about the head in my own children's school whom I knew quite well. Although she loved the job, she told me that the big difference between being a deputy and a head was that all eyes and ears are on you and *the burden of responsibility never goes away.* Even when you are lying on a beach on holiday, the responsibility is there, always creeping up on you just as you begin to relax. Every word you say will be picked up on and dissected.

3   The head in my previous school had left me in charge of the school for three weeks while he took part in an educational study trip. It was frightening how much you can change the ethos of a school in a few short weeks. I didn't wreck the place but there were certainly some subtle differences around the school which he noticed on his return. It brought home to me *the influence – and, dare I say it, power – a head can hold.*

4   I was a short, bald Italian man with a strong Scottish accent. I had struggled with dyslexia at school and university (until computers came along and transformed my life – but that is another story). Even though I had been successful as a deputy head, I couldn't shake off the memory of an assistant head who, when showing me around the school for the first time, led me into the staffroom and announced in a loud but cheery voice: 'If you're wondering who this funny little man is, whom I have been showing around, this is your new deputy head.' With a smile, she then led me off to meet some students, oblivious to my bruised ego. In short, I had a very bad case of *imposter syndrome* (something I have never really been able to shake off but have learned to live with, as we will see in Cog 1.2).

That first training day in September was top of the charts when it comes to scary. I had met most of the staff during the previous term, but not formally. This would be my first moment as a proper head teacher. The fact that the school had been put into special measures following a damning inspection report didn't worry me. Nor did that year's exam results – placing it as the seventh lowest performing school in the country – make me want to run. Nor the fact that it had the highest exclusion figures in the country. Not even that it had been closed and was due to reopen with the same staff and students as an academy. We were to move into a new building for the first time, with all the unknowns that would bring, but I knew I would cope with that. Just for good measure, there was also a police order in the local area that banned groups of more than three young people from gathering at any one time due to running battles with rival gangs on the streets outside the school. All of this was fine; I would handle it.

Nope, the things that worried me were all about me, me, me.

Perhaps you have decided that you want to be the head of a school or maybe a head of department. You feel ready for the role and the responsibility that goes with it. What you may not be so ready for is how best to handle the focus that will be on you constantly. How will you cope with almost everyone agreeing with you on a daily basis (to your face at least)? How will you manage being the centre of attention? How aware will you be of any changes in your own behaviour following your first successes or failures? And if the adulation is all going your way, how will you respond when someone disagrees with you? Will you recognise when your behaviour begins to change at home or with friends? These are all the little things that could tip the ethos in your school or department in one direction or another.

What I am describing here concerns the ego. The Latin word for 'I', it is often misinterpreted and misused. The standard definition for the term ego is 'Someone's ... sense of their own worth. For example, if someone has a large ego, they think they are very important and valuable.'[1] However, the term was first brought into common usage in the translations of Sigmund Freud.[2] Freud described the ego as 'that part of the id which has been modified by the direct influence of the external world'.[3] The id can described as 'the impulsive (and unconscious) part of our psyche which responds directly and immediately to basic urges, needs, and desires'.[4] For example, when babies are born they are all id; as the baby matures, so does the ego in order to modify behaviours according to reality.

In the standard sense, I used to think that I didn't have much of an ego because I had a million insecurities and rarely pushed myself to go for promotions. What I

---

1   See https://www.collinsdictionary.com/dictionary/english/ego.
2   Freud actually used the German word 'es' to describe the part of the self that is responsible for decision-making: see Lauren Guilbault, 'What's the Best Way to Define Ego?', *BetterHelp* (7 May 2021). Available at: https://www.betterhelp.com/advice/willpower/whats-the-best-way-to-define-ego.
3   Sigmund Freud, 'The Ego and the Id', in *The Standard Edition of the Complete Psychological Works of Sigmund Freud, Volume XIX (1923–1925): The Ego and the Id and Other Works* (London: Hogarth Press, 1961 [1923]), pp. 1–66 at p. 25. Cited in Saul McLeod, 'Id, Ego and Superego', *Simply Psychology* (25 September 2019). Available at: https://www.simplypsychology.org/psyche.html.
4   McLeod, 'Id, Ego and Superego'.

actually had, if we use Freud's definition, was a healthy ego. As a head of department, I remember once telling a colleague that I would never go for a senior leadership role. My colleague's reply was, 'You should only think about going for the next stage when you feel ready.' This was my ego working as it should. An unhealthy ego that is not in check can lead to poorly judged actions – for example, we may refuse to be proven wrong in an argument with someone to whom we feel superior. Even though we know we are mistaken, we may argue to the bitter end. Conversely, if we feel overly inferior, we may give up too easily, even though we know we are right.

It would be fair to say that all prospective heads have a degree of egotism which enables them to feel confident, strong and, quite possibly, superior enough to apply for headships. This self-belief may stem from a healthy ego which draws on past experience or from an unshakeable and/or irrational self-assurance which may arise from an unhealthy ego. This elevated ego may have its advantages but they are limited.

The problem arises when we want to do it *our* way and close our ears to advice from others. After all, we have come into the job wanting to lead a school or department with a degree of autonomy. Many of you may have spent most of your professional life thinking that you could do it better and criticised every little thing that every head has ever asked you to do. However, during your time as a teacher and as a middle or senior leader, if you have learned anything, it should be that we are only human – everyone makes mistakes. We need to listen to advice and weigh up all sides of a debate before deciding on a course of action. Easy to say, but the unhealthy part of our ego can grasp the upper hand, resulting in us pushing ahead with our own beliefs and ignoring other voices.

This is where the tension comes in. A certain degree of ego is necessary when it comes to leadership. Someone has to have enough belief in themselves to make the final decision. In an emergency situation, we cannot wait for a democratic decision-making process to occur before any action is taken. Having said that, it is important to remember that ego shouldn't be the driver when it comes to making decisions. As soon as you put yourself on a pedestal, you lose touch with the ebb and flow of day-to-day life in your school.

Let us take an example which affected me during a heatwave in 2018. With temperatures rising above 30 degrees, the pressure was on us to allow students to wear their PE kits to school (four weeks before the end of term). Some schools were relenting and the national media had picked up on the story. My first reaction was to say no: everyone should remain in normal school uniform – including staff, who were starting to wear flip-flops and other attire which were not what I would have expected in a professional-looking workforce. While some of the senior team and staff were in favour of relaxing the rules, many had started to argue otherwise. Parents were also beginning to inundate us with requests. The easy option would have been to give in and let the students come into school in their PE kit. However, I remained consistent with my initial reaction and insisted that our students continue to wear their uniforms, albeit without a blazer if they wished. The heatwave carried on for the remainder of the term, but within a few days of the initial demands being made, things had died down and the students continued to come to school in full uniform.

Why did I stick to my initial reaction? Was this an unhealthy side of my ego getting the better of me or was it something else? To answer this question it is important to consider my thought processes during this situation. Not only were other schools allowing their students to wear PE kits, but I also had the pressure of many parents and staff demanding that I should relent. However, I was aware there were still four weeks to go until the end of term, and we had worked very hard that year to ensure everyone was in uniform. Parents respected our uniform policy and I didn't want it to be undermined. I was also conscious that the media push these types of stories and then they disappear quickly. Finally, I felt that many would respect the decision to stay true to our uniform policy and I certainly didn't want to set a precedent for going back on policies.

If my resolve had been purely dependent on egotism, I probably wouldn't have stood firm. However, what served me well in this instance and caused my healthy ego to work appropriately was gut instinct based on experience. There is much debate regarding the worth of gut instinct. In *Blink*, Malcolm Gladwell describes how a snap decision or judgement is often much more effective than a decision based on a rigorous analysis of the facts.[5] While he also highlights the fallibility of this approach, there is much merit in what he says. When I first became a head, I used to always say when something didn't go as planned that 'I wish I'd listened to my gut feeling.' Frequently, I knew the decision I was making was wrong but I went with what the majority were telling me to do.

....

5   Malcolm Gladwell, *Blink: The Power of Thinking without Thinking* (London: Penguin, 2005).

Gladwell helped me to appreciate how important it is to listen to your gut, but I have also learned how vital it is to rationalise why your gut feels this way. If you can't justify your feelings and vocalise them to others then perhaps it is your unhealthy ego taking over. In summary: be aware of your ego. If you don't nurture its healthy side, it can make you pretty unpopular and lose you a lot of respect. It can give you the self-belief to make strong decisions, but make sure you back them up with a rationale based on experience.

Cog 1.2: Creating that first impression

In the previous cog, we considered the dangers of an inflated ego. We now need to consider how an inflated ego can manifest itself when we seek to create a good first impression with the staff we will lead.

Being aware of our unconscious insecurities

Any change in leadership brings with it a degree of uncertainty, so staff will need to feel confident in their head (or any other potential leader) if they are going to buy into the ethos that the school community or department is trying to develop. The last thing anyone working in a school wants to pick up from a leader is inde-cisiveness or a lack of confidence, therefore having an understanding of, and control over, your own insecurities is a prerequisite, especially when commencing a new role.

Back around the turn of the century, I applied for a deputy head position at the City Academy, Bristol, after we as a family decided to move from the south-east of London. I was a senior teacher at the time in a fairly challenging school and had been promoted internally. I had been successful in the role and felt relatively secure. I had the usual self-doubts but applied for the deputy role nevertheless. I was successful in gaining an interview and felt excited as I drove over for the two-day process. I liked the school and thought I would get on well with the head; however, by lunchtime insecurity had started to creep in. The other applicants were all very self-assured men – and a lot taller than me. This was another school in difficult circumstances and I began to feel that I might not be up to it. My self-doubt continued to grow to the extent that, by the end of the first day, I told the head I didn't think I was right for the job. He asked me to think about it overnight and call him in the morning.

I had so thoroughly convinced myself I couldn't do the job that I drove all the way back to London. I called a consultant friend, who has always been my educational guru and guide (we all need one!), who told me in no uncertain terms that I was being ridiculous and ordered me back to Bristol. The head seemed pleased to see me (although he might have thought differently had he known about the nocturnal drive to London) and at the end of the second day – to my complete amazement – he offered me the job. I gratefully accepted and have never looked back.

This experience brings to mind the psychoanalyst Melanie Klein, whose work inspired many of the theories we will look at in Chapter 3:

If we look at our adult world from the viewpoint of its roots in infancy, we gain an insight into the way our mind, our habits, and our views have been built up from the earliest infantile phantasies and emotions to the most complex and sophisticated adult manifestations. There is one more conclusion to be drawn, which is that nothing that ever existed in the unconscious completely loses its influence on the personality.[6]

We all carry insecurities, however deeply buried, and it is so easy to allow these to come to the fore when we are faced with stressful situations. During the interview process, I felt a pressing need to be something I wasn't. I know it was irrational, but as Klein intimates, our experiences (especially recurrent ones) of childhood and adolescence remain with us. These traces of our younger, developing selves remain as unconscious fragments and influence our actions. In this case, I had wrongly perceived a subtext manifested by the presence of four six-foot-plus males alongside five-and-a-half-foot me. On reflection, I had recalled similar

---

6   Melanie Klein, 'Our Adult World and Its Roots in Infancy', in *Envy and Gratitude and Other Works 1946–1963* (London: Vintage, 1997 [1959]), pp. 247–263 at p. 262.

situations in my own past where I had backed out. This led me to believe that, in this instance too, I was not the person for the job and therefore could not be my authentic self. It was for this reason that I withdrew. However, when I returned the next day, with my friend's words ringing in my ears, I came back as myself and was rewarded with a new job.

A similar situation occurred during the months between successfully interviewing for my first headship and taking up the role: the self-doubt steadily grew as the new term approached. Having listened to me bleat on about all my inadequacies for a few months, a fellow deputy head said, 'For God's sake, Armando, just be yourself.' She was so very right. It has been my most important mantra since becoming a head and it has served me well.

These examples illustrate how a lack of self-confidence can create barriers for ourselves, which not only damage us but ultimately affect the confidence of those we lead. We can overcome these obstacles by recognising, acknowledging and accepting those times when we are being flooded by negative emotions.

Those who are unable to tolerate feelings of insecurity can become inflexible and defensive at the cost of losing authenticity and integrity. To overcome this, we must always remain curious about the situation in which we find ourselves and possible paths to follow, and then draw on the positive life experiences that have contributed to us becoming a leader. These tools can help to develop the resilience and the strength we all possess to overcome those times when the imposter within us tries to take over.

Your first meeting with staff

As a head teacher or a head of department, the first time you meet all your staff together is always hard because it is when they will form their judgement about you. With every eye on you, this is when you make clear your values and long-term intentions and, if it is the initial meeting of the autumn term, clarify the priorities and aims for the year ahead. Whether it is the first time you are talking to the staff or not, as heads we should meet with our staff at the beginning of every year. Every presentation you give to staff is almost as important as the first one. Not only will there be new members of staff but (as we will discuss later) repetition and reinforcement are essential when it comes to school leadership.

Think about how judgemental we are when we meet someone. Research on the subject tends to agree that it takes very little time to form an opinion and it is very difficult to change that opinion.[7] It is vital, therefore, that who you are comes across as quickly as possible, and in the best way possible, before that initial opinion manifests itself in a decision being made.

Some things you might want to consider when meeting all your staff for the first time (before you dive into what you actually want to say) include:

- Show that you know and value them as a staff – for example, 'I've heard so much from [my predecessor, the chair of governors, the executive principal, etc.] about how [hard-working, welcoming, friendly, etc.] you are as a staff.'

- Don't be afraid to show some of your own vulnerabilities. It indicates that you are honest about your weaknesses and subconsciously tells your audience that they can do this too. This is especially important if they are in need of support. A little humour can help too.

- Start how you mean to go on, with honesty and a caring approach. If the job ahead is going to be a tough one – for instance, if the school needs to come out of special measures – then let your staff know that you will be making some tough decisions. Emphasise that you will always be transparent, that you will consult with them and, above all, that you will be accessible. The staff will know what is on the cards well before even you know it. It is called rumour and gossip. It is better to confirm than deny.

- Remind staff that you always value feedback. They need to know that you cannot improve a school effectively without feedback about what needs improving and what is working or not working well. It is about creating a culture where there isn't a fear that people will be judged for saying something negative to the head.

Preparing for your first presentation

Whether or not to use a script to support your first presentation will depend on your ability and level of comfort when it comes to speaking to an audience.

---

7   Eric Wargo, 'How Many Seconds to a First Impression?', *Association for Psychological Science* (1 July 2006). Available at: https://www.psychologicalscience.org/observer/how-many-seconds-to-a-first-impression.

Scripted presentations ensure that you don't stray from the points you are trying to make, go off-piste and regret later something you have said. Equally, a script can dilute your passion and authenticity and may not engage the listener in the same way; we speak differently to how we write.

Prompt notes are an improvement on a script but, personally, I never feel as inspired when I watch speakers with cards. However, for your first speech or presentation you should do whatever makes you feel most comfortable. I have always used slides and complementary pictures as they help to embed the message into your audience's memory but don't distract from what you are saying. For example, I wanted to show how at a particular moment the school was on a knife edge, so I displayed a picture of a mountain arête with steep cliff edges on either side. The picture also showed how the ridge would rise and fall to illustrate the good and bad days we would have. I then displayed a picture of a mountain with gentle rounded slopes, which demonstrated that, in time and with good systems and processes, we might still have good and bad days, but we would feel more secure and less likely to fall off the edge. If you are using slides, bullet points can be a useful tool to help you remember what to say (although try not to use too many). Overall, I agree with Richard Branson when he says, 'your story should take centre stage. Slides complement the story; they don't replace the story.'[8]

If you find the prospect of a presentation daunting, then practise well beforehand so you appear genuine and natural. Anyone can promise the earth when reading from a pre-prepared speech; however, if what you say is spontaneous it will feel authentic to the listener. Based on my own experiences, the most salient guiding principles to making a good presentation include:

- Keep it simple and cover only a few topics.

- Make it personal – stories are always more interesting.

- Talk with passion, so focus on things you feel really strongly about.

- Walk about and make eye contact. Don't hide behind a lectern.

- A bit of humility goes a long way. You need your staff, so don't forget that they can help you.

....

8   Carmine Gallo, 'Richard Branson: "If It Can't Fit On the Back of an Envelope, It's Rubbish (an Interview)"', *Forbes* (22 October 2012). Available at: https://www.forbes.com/sites/carminegallo/2012/10/22/richard-branson-if-it-cant-fit-on-the-back-of-an-envelope-its-rubbish-interview/?sh=409934b31ae9.

● Limit the presentation to 30–40 minutes if you are a dynamic speaker. If you are a less confident presenter (be honest with yourself – it might not be a strength), then cut it to 20 minutes.

The main body of your first presentation

If you commence your new role as a head at the beginning of the school year, there will be the usual business to conduct, such as welcoming new staff and reflecting on the previous year's exam results. This should come after any introductions and your main presentation. First and foremost, the staff will want to get to know you.

If we assume that you are about to inherit a 'normal' school, with no major concerns, the main areas you need to cover are as follows:

● How you intend to operate as a head – for example, how visible you will be and how accessible. I have always let it be known to staff that if my door is open, they are welcome to pop in and ask me anything; if my door is closed, and they need to see me urgently, they should ask my PA.

● Your expectations. Be truthful about these: if you try to win friends by softening your stance and then up your expectations later, you will be in trouble. I made this mistake in my first school as a head, where I subsequently found it difficult to smarten the staff dress code and improve punctuality to lessons after break or lunch.

● Your aims and vision and why you think this will make a difference. This is the meat of your presentation and needs to be strong. As with your expectations, it is easy to go light on this; however, people want to hear what you believe in and gain some insight into the direction you might be taking the school. We will focus on vision in Chapter 2.

● Highlight a few things you would like to focus on and improve in the school initially. This will reinforce the perception that you know what you are talking about and are familiar with the school. Make sure you do your homework. Your chair of governors, executive head, local authority or school inspection report will help you with this. One method I have adopted is to always start the academic year with an aim for that year – for example: 'XXXX School 2019–2020: adequate to good.'[9]

Following your speech or presentation, aim to engage and consult with your staff in various ways. This will provide you with a series of openings to get to know them. Strengths, weaknesses, opportunities and threats (SWOT) type activities will help you to gauge the temperature of the school and give staff a chance to voice their concerns, hopes and fears. The activity is primarily one of self-reflection, but it also makes clear that you are looking for staff who will work with you to take the school to the next level.

This is sufficient to create a good impression on your first day. By this point the staff will:

- Know a little about you and hopefully have seen the human side of you.
- Know that you will be approachable.
- Understand that you mean business: you know the school and what needs to be done.
- Have been given the opportunity to reflect by themselves and with others on your intentions.
- Have given you some feedback.

All that remains for you to do is to meet your SLT and to be visible. Try to meet as many staff as possible informally on that first day (or two days if it is a two-day INSET).

One more word of warning: try to avoid running training sessions on the first day, unless there is a specific activity that you know is engaging, worthwhile and relevant for staff, or if there are specific operational details you want the staff to know. Otherwise, do one of two things: (1) allow your senior team to lead the activities, as it is a chance to see them in action, or (2) if you are unsure about the team, it is a safer bet to have one INSET day and give the staff time to prepare for a subsequent INSET day. You can always hold another training day early in the new term (if you had a say on the training days before you arrived).

---

9   I first saw this used by Steve Taylor, the then head of Bristol Metropolitan Academy.

Cog 1.3: Act the behaviours you want to see – modelling

This cog contains more than any other on describing the outward-facing behaviours that embody the school ethos. I learned most about modelling certain behaviours from a previous head teacher, Ray Priest, when I was one of his deputies. He was always out and about with a smile on his face, lifting the school when it was in its hardest moments. I used to naively question many of his practices, but later on I learned how important they were. What follows are a few strategies that I have adopted in all my subsequent schools from day one.

Being highly visible

Ray was rarely in his office because he was always walking around the school. He used to ask the leadership team to be visible too but with mixed success. Some used to complain that they had other urgent or important work to do, and most often they probably did, but as I soon found out, the benefits of being visible outweighed this.

Many would argue that spending much of your time as a senior leader out and about is a poor use of their skills and expertise. The school is paying these individuals a lot of money to develop a strong ethos and achieve high outcomes for the students. However, I maintain that being highly visible – including litter picking, if need be – is an essential part of creating a positive school ethos that is conducive to raising student outcomes. Being visible reduces incidents of bad behaviour, and fewer incidents lessens the number of interruptions to the work you need to do. More importantly, it results in fewer distractions in the classroom.

However, there is a difficult balancing act ahead should you decide to follow this path. There are two aspects to consider. The first concerns work–life balance. If you are out in the corridors and classrooms during every lesson, when do you complete the other work you need to do and answer all those emails building up in your inbox? Rotas can help: insisting that members of the SLT are out and about during their allotted times, rather than simply being on call, is essential. It is not just about answering duty calls and keeping a lid on behaviour, but also about showing staff that there is always a senior presence around, popping into rooms to say hello and looking at what the students are learning. Some staff dislike this (often those who need the most support) but the majority like to see the SLT showing an interest in what is going on.

One way that I fit in some paperwork during the day is to sit in an open space and work on a laptop. But even so, I still like to be in the corridors between lessons and to have at least one walk-around during every period. Lesson changeovers are a time when everyone should be out. Teachers should be at their doors not only to greet their students, but also to chivvy them along to their next class, and all the SLT need to be around if possible. We will return to behaviour in Chapter 3, but more than anything, this practice maintains a well-ordered and calm school with consistently good standards of teaching and learning.

The second aspect to consider is authenticity and staff perceptions. Authenticity is a recurring theme in this book in respect to leadership. Your day-to-day, visible actions and interactions are where your staff and students will judge how genuine you are in relation to the level of care you have for them and the school. Consistency is key in the examples that follow. If you only perform these activities when other people are around, they will never become habit-forming and you are in danger of staff noticing that your seemingly altruistic actions are simply a shallow form of PR.

Litter picking

Ray would always pick litter. And not just one or two pieces here and there; he would go round with a bin liner and fill it at lunchtime. I had always picked up the odd bit of litter if I spotted some in the corridor, but I thought that what Ray did was well beyond what a head should do. At the time I thought it was undignified, but I was so wrong.

Picking up litter sends a message to staff and students. At first, they look at you as if you are mad, but little by little more and more of the students will pick up a piece of litter for you before you reach it. They seem to appreciate it because it shows that you care about them and the school. They certainly don't look at you as if you are demeaning yourself. Sometimes I think young people are a lot more perceptive than adults in this way. Having said that, some staff also begin to model the practice (and not just when they think I am looking). As an extra bonus, it cheers up the premises staff!

Remaining upbeat, especially when times are hard

Ray would always be smiling in the corridors. I would run to tell him about some horrendous situation that was developing, and he would simply smile, keep it light and joke casually about it as we walked towards the incident. It often used to drive me mad but he would always be listening.

Staff and students need to feel safe and looked after, especially if the school is challenging. If the senior team or I had walked around the school with a look of doom plastered all over our faces, the school would have never lifted. It would have become okay for everyone else to look that way too, and that would soon rub off on the students whose insecurities would begin to play out.

Be aware of your facial expressions; it is so easy to walk around wearing a frown. You will soon find that both staff and students notice what is not the norm and may ask you what is wrong. If they do begin to do this, it highlights another facet of the ethos we should be aiming to create – one of trust, where anyone can give you feedback without fear of recrimination.

Never run to a fight

Fights between students can break out in any school. If there is a staff presence around, the conflict can be quickly de-escalated, but I always advise staff not to run to the incident. We will cover fights and how to deal with them in Cog 3.5, but let us assume for the moment that you have been told that a fight is about to start or see one brewing. If you sprint towards it, 50 students will follow. If three other teachers do the same thing, coming from different directions, you suddenly have 200 students congregating around the two potential fighters.

It would frustrate Ray to see members of staff snowballing a potentially containable situation into something much more serious by running to the fight and wading in without any thought to their own safety or that of children being tossed out the way. True, it will stem from good intentions but, sadly, without the desired outcomes. In each of my schools, we have spent a lot of time looking at this issue with staff and discussing alternative scenarios.

Remain calm in an emergency or when there is a high state of alert

If the head or an SLT member is running around in an emergency (or possible emergency) and barking orders indiscriminately, then others will panic and noise levels will rise. Here are a few ways to model good practice:

- No matter how bad it is, approach every situation in a composed and measured way. If you are an experienced leader, you will know instinctively what to do.

- Ask students quietly not to gather around if someone is injured. Don't threaten a student who doesn't listen – it will only add to the list of things you have to deal with. You can deal with offending individuals later.

- Reassure everyone in a calm voice; it is often worth playing things down with the onlookers, even if it is a serious incident.

- Take control of the situation by giving tasks to responsible students and/or staff if they are around – for example, to support a limb or ask the office to call 999. Again, this is best done in a calm and considered way.

Never walk past a misdemeanour

I always tell new staff that the best way to gain respect from students is to show that you care, and one of the most honest and appreciated ways of doing this is never to walk past a misdemeanour. I go on to say that if you make a point of spotting one thing on your way from your class to the staffroom, and then follow it up, the students will begin to notice a real change in how their peers respond to and behave around you. If every member of staff adheres to this principle, the students will soon realise that there are certain things they will never get away with. The more we use the phrase, 'That's not how we do things here,' the greater the chance of it becoming true.

It is so easy to let go something that appears trivial – for example, a missing tie (if that is part of your uniform code) or someone dropping a piece of litter. When you are in a rush, there is the temptation to disregard it just this once. However, that is a steep slippery slope and one you should avoid at all costs. Furthermore, the head cannot be the only person doing this; it is something that you need to keep repeating to your SLT, and when you are sure they are all following this, then to your middle leaders. Trying to get all the staff to do this from the outset will likely frustrate you, so it is better to build up the practice in small segments at a time.

Voice and language

It is amazing how difficult it is to maintain standards around voice and language. Again, it comes down to modelling by your SLT and, hopefully, your middle leaders too.

The two key things to remember here are: (1) never raise your voice in a way that can be construed as aggressive and (2) never use language that can be read as insulting, sarcastic, demeaning or derogatory. This needs to be explored with staff constantly (we will explore this in more detail in Chapter 3) but, for now, from a head's point of view (and especially a head joining a new school), it is crucial that you establish these standards from day one. If not, your workload will increase with every term that goes by. In my schools, failure to follow these two principles has been the basis for most complaints from parents and, unfortunately, disciplinary procedures taken against members of staff.

This is hard when staff are tired, perhaps stressed and have been on the receiving end of a mouthful of hurtful abuse from a student. However, this is something that all staff have to be aware of and that will always be followed up if a staff member is found to have acted unprofessionally.

Confident and professional demeanour

We are good at what we do and when you send your children to us, you can trust us to look after them well and give them a really good all-round education.

The statement above is something I always say to prospective parents. This is a simple way of describing what it means to be a professional. Professional status goes hand in hand with trust and the training necessary to gain that trust. We trust doctors to the extent that we place our lives in their hands; similarly, we entrust our children to the care of teachers.

It can be easy to lose this level of confidence when working in a challenging school. For example, I have come across staff with a laissez-faire approach to the students – for example, cajoling them into working but with an underlying element of fear that if you push them too hard there will be a backlash. In classrooms, 'busy' work takes place rather than meaningful learning experiences, and in the corridors a certain level of bad language by students to one another is tolerated.

It is therefore essential that the head teacher and heads of department exude an air of quiet confidence and have high expectations of their staff and students. If this professional demeanour is maintained, it will gradually seep into the behaviours of all staff at every level in the school and, in time, it will become the perceived norm for any new members of staff to the school.

I have always tried to encourage staff in my senior team to model the professional behaviours they want to see; however, I am also conscious that we don't go too far and create a stuffy and unfriendly environment where students don't feel cared for. The approach we use is to say, 'We don't do this at ... ' or 'This is how we do this at ... ', but at the same time we try to maintain a kind and caring ethos.

This is not an easy task in a challenging school. Staff can be pulled in many directions on a daily basis, whether it is through a poor set of grades, a lousy inspection or unruly behaviour. It is difficult to maintain this degree of professional confidence but it is crucial that we do so. The communities we serve deserve nothing less.

To sum up this cog, the responsibility rests on the head teacher to set the standards and to model them continuously. The head needs to ensure that their senior team does the same, and gradually to work with others until the expected behaviours become habitual throughout the school. It is a top-down approach but that is the nature of modelling – we tend to look to those above us to see how it should be done.

The actions and practices described in this cog are the early behaviours that have to be exhibited if a school is to begin to improve its ethos and, ultimately, the quality of its teaching, learning and outcomes. Some of this may sound slightly calculated, but as your actions become habits, you will become less self-conscious and they will begin to feel more natural. Having a team around you supporting you and modelling the same behaviours will make the transition easier for everyone and speed up the process of these behaviours and actions becoming the norm for your school.

Cog 1.4: Design a road map

A road map that describes what you will do and when is an indispensable tool when it comes to school improvement. In effect, it is a long-term plan (which we will look at in more detail in Chapter 2), but for a head or even a head of department who is new to post and under pressure to make many changes, a road map is the best way to maintain control and ensure the integrity of the ethos you are trying to develop.

Having fulfilled almost all of my senior leader roles in academies from their inception, I have witnessed the immense pressure that schools can be put under to improve quickly. The one thing I have learned from this is that you cannot turn around a school overnight.

Eastern High in Cardiff was put into special measures just before I took up my post. The media were constantly printing stories that created alarm in the community, which in turn placed the local authority in a difficult position as the Welsh government began to raise questions. A few months into the role, I had a meeting with the local authority director and a well-regarded government officer from England. The government officer literally thumped his fist on the table several times, exclaiming that I was not moving the school forward fast enough and that I had to move underperforming staff on more quickly. The six members of staff who were following capability procedures and the SLT restructure I was in the midst of, were not progressing fast enough. After berating me for 20 minutes or so, and before I could so much as blink with astonishment, he left with a swish and never returned.

Although the diatribe was pointless, the meeting wasn't. It spurred me into action. For years, I had been subject to the same unrealistic expectations with regard to timescales for school improvement. However, I could also see that the argument was a fair one: every minute the school was in its current dire position, we were letting down children.

This is the hard fact that has to be faced when attempting to pull a school out of a failing situation. Logic dictates that speed should be of the essence, which can force schools to put in place strategies and procedures that are not sustainable over the long term, and which can result in any or all of the following: huge deficits, unhappy/striking staff, behaviour spiralling out of control as students reject draconian rules (which can then lead to high exclusion rates), unhappy parents and falling rolls. In short, this strategy may create a situation where initial successes are offset by a downward spiral a few years later. Consider the following implementation chart, on page 28.

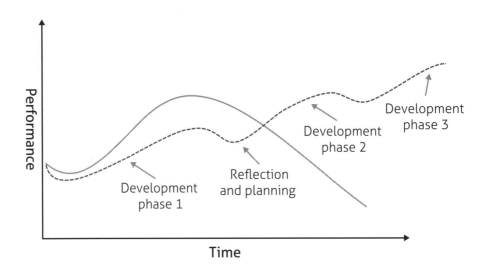

The solid line is a worst-case scenario: the school in challenging circumstances may have an improvement plan in place but is driven by quick-win outcomes and little consideration for the stable foundations that every school requires, resulting in some or all of the outcomes listed in the previous paragraph. Schools in easier circumstances, with reasonably good outcomes, are more likely to follow the dotted line: after the usual implementation dip there is sustained improvement, with points in the school's development where reflection and new development takes place. The school may experience a small dip at these junctures but the overall trend is upwards.

Schools in challenging circumstances that have gone into (or are about to go into) special measures are under extreme pressure to improve and so fall into the quick-win trap. It is not the purpose of this book to name and shame schools that have followed this path, as undoubtedly those in charge will have faced enormous pressure to improve, but it is worth reflecting on why some schools fail – in particular, those once-lauded institutions that suddenly find themselves in dire straits.

Quick-win strategies that don't work

It is worth highlighting some of the pressures that school leaders can come under and explore some of the relatively quick and potentially easier ways to show those who are placing you under pressure (along with the wider community) that the school is on an upward trajectory. New heads are especially vulnerable to following one or more of these routes as they try to prove their worth as a head teacher.

1. Moving on underperforming staff

The three schools I have led have all had a high proportion of underperforming staff. Imagine the consequences of approaching this in an insensitive way – identifying all those underachieving and putting them on capability procedures straight away. This would take up an enormous amount of time and resources, and consequently there would be less capacity for tackling other areas, such as bad behaviour or staff development. In addition, acting too quickly before the staff know and trust you can lead to mass discontent. If this leads to poor morale (that dreaded phrase), before you know it you have union action, grievances and even more underperforming staff to contend with.

If you do succeed in moving on a large number of underperforming staff, and you and the school are still in one piece, how will you replace them? Recruitment to a school in challenging circumstances is not easy. We will return to this in Cog 4.4.

2. Pouring all your resources into achieving good Year 11 results

Why not focus on GCSE grades? If results rise, those to whom you are accountable will be satisfied and parents might begin to have faith in the school. You might even fool the inspectors into believing the school is good and going in the right direction (although it is unlikely). It is such an easy thing to do (in theory) but, at best, it is a short-term strategy. Everyone wants improving results and students deserve the very best, especially if in previous years they have had a raw deal. This is all true but it is all about balance. Unfortunately, maintaining this balance is probably one of the hardest things I have had to do as a head teacher: things can easily get out of hand.

For example, in my first headship, I put a huge amount of time and resources into improving results and, as previously mentioned, our results were good. However, when those successful Year 11 students had left, we turned around to look at the next cohort and stared into a chasm. The Year 10s had been neglected; indeed, our capacity to provide interventions in all other year groups had been diverted to Year 11. The result was a year of monumental effort to ensure that the new Year 11 at least matched the success of the previous year.

My team and I were fortunate to have realised this sufficiently early on, so we opted to accept lower results that year in order to ensure that each year group were receiving the attention they required. It took a few years to achieve this but it was worth it. If we hadn't done so, we may have managed a couple of years with good results, but the bad practice would have inevitably caught up with us. I also wonder how other aspects of the school we had neglected in the meantime would have fared.

3. Behaviour, behaviour, behaviour

I have certainly heard this statement a few times: 'If we sort out behaviour quickly, it'll impress visitors and then give us time to work on everything else.' And: 'We need to get rid of the worst offenders; it'll send a message to students and staff.' I am not going to spend long on this one, as we will look at behaviour in much more detail in Chapter 3.

Let us return to my inspirational moment, which followed the table-thumping episode in my office. I am a fairly calm person and outwardly I managed to preserve my mild-mannered persona, but I must confess that a few expletives ran around my head. It was then that my inspiration came: what I needed was a big 'Back off' chart on the door of my office that any visitor could read before they came in to tell me to do things faster.

Okay, the chart wouldn't be headed 'Back off'; instead, I opted for a subtler message: 'The Eastern High Road Map'. The chart outlined all the areas we would aim to improve over the next four years and give timescales for each aspect. If I was new to headship, I probably wouldn't have had the confidence to tell people that I couldn't do it any quicker. It was only the experience of many improvement processes in my career that I was able to identify with self-assurance the capacity we had to improve things and at what rate we would tackle them.

In retrospect, I could have done this just as easily during my first headship and I would have been praised for having clear and strategic leadership. There was no rocket science involved in drawing up the chart. As a team, we considered every aspect of the school we needed to improve, what resources we might require and how long it might take to achieve. In this way, we were able to work out roughly how many areas we had the capacity and finances to address at any one time and prioritise accordingly the tasks/activities we had identified.

The chart was divided into four columns which represented the four pillars underpinning the vision for our school (which we will look at in Cog 2.6). On the left side was a timeline divided into five time zones:

1   **Discovering.** This covered my first two terms at Eastern High. It involved an investigation into what systems and processes were in place and then evaluating their quality.

2   **Foundations.** The next stage involved prioritising the essential aspects of the school to be improved and developing appropriate systems.

3   **Emerging.** This involved testing the systems we had put in place and embedding them into the day-to-day life of the school.

4   **Growth.** By this point, it was anticipated that we would come out of special measures and would begin to move away from the functional systems that ensured stability. This stage was, and still is, about transforming the school from good to outstanding (or excellent, as Estyn[10] refers to it). It represents the growth in confidence we hoped to achieve.

5   **Flourishing.** This was a reminder that flourishing is a goal for our students and for all of us as an institution and community.

The chart became an invaluable tool. Initially, it was on the door to my office, but I was constantly taking it down to go through it in detail with every table-thumper who popped in for a visit (which was often). Staff appreciated its clarity and transparency and both current and prospective parents gained a clear understanding of the direction in which we were taking the school. For all stakeholders, it seemed to act as a calming agent for the high state of alert the school was in at the time. Maybe it was our actions that reassured people (I cannot say for certain), but I like to think it was our road map that kick-started the school's recovery and ensured we developed a school ethos in a consistent and sustainable way.

---

10 Estyn is the education and training inspectorate for Wales.

Cog 1.5: Avoiding distractions

Initiative overload

As a head starting in an unfamiliar location and school, it is all too easy to fall into the 'yes' trap. When I first moved to Eastern High, I was inundated with requests, invitations and offers of help (or special discount offers). Most of them were worthwhile individually but collectively they spelled disaster. I was new to Cardiff and Wales and new to working in a local authority (having worked in academies for the previous 12 years), so I wasn't familiar with what were the most important, urgent or beneficial requests and offers of support. I told the assistant director of education that I would make a list of everything that came in (a time-consuming task in itself but a good investment nevertheless) and asked if she would look at the list and let me know which ones had three-line whips attached to them and which ones I could put to one side. I already had my own opinion (ignore everything!), but I wanted to highlight the extent to which a head can be pulled in a hundred different directions by well-meaning initiatives.

I worked in one school in my early years which was in very difficult circumstances and consequently looked for the panacea for school improvement. As teachers, we were subject to a dozen different training initiatives: various trainers and companies were invited to present their one-stop-shop cures for all the behavioural issues in the school. Individually, there were some fantastic ideas and methods, and had the school stuck to one and embedded it fully perhaps we would have seen a positive change in the culture of the school. Unfortunately, nothing was given enough time and we were left to try out different initiatives for short periods, resulting in no consistency across the school.

It is so tempting for a school in difficult circumstances to pounce on the potential cure-alls that come its way. Imagine, for example, that you are presented with the following offers: three different training sessions laid on by the local authority for specific subject heads (two in the morning and one in the afternoon) and a science conference for up to half of your Year 11 students. You cannot miss the training sessions for fear of losing out on vital information and risk the school falling even further behind, and you cannot miss the latter for fear that students from schools that do attend will achieve better science results.

However, to participate in the training events the school will have to find cover for three heads of department, and to enable the Year 11 students to attend the science event you will need to find cover supervision for up to four or five staff members (they may not be teachers necessarily but, nevertheless, they are members of staff who have other important jobs to fulfil in the school). On top of this, there is the organisational time involved to consider. If you have a six-lesson day, it could equate to between 30 and 40 lessons being covered that week. You might reduce this by sending teachers who teach Year 11 to the event, but at best this will only reduce the supply cover by a couple of lessons.

Getting the balance right

Every school is bombarded with opportunities to participate but it comes at a cost. Initially, there may be a net gain due to the advantages that external activities can bring, but get involved in too many too often and you will reach a tipping point.

This may seem obvious but when you are new in post and want to make an impression, the temptation is to say yes to everyone. It is easy to turn away companies (charities are a little harder), but it is extremely difficult to say no to requests and invitations from local authorities or your MAT leadership team. If you are in a school in challenging circumstances, then refusing support becomes even more difficult. It can be a no-win situation. If you accept all the support offered, you are in danger of scuppering your carefully planned timetable for improvement. However, if you turn the support down and the school doesn't improve, then you won't be long in that particular school!

This situation requires you to draw on your experience and leadership qualities to justify your decision to participate or not in certain activities. Here are a few things to consider when it comes to external activities and support:

- Do those to whom the school is accountable expect participation? Will it be a huge embarrassment to the school if you don't? If the answer is yes, then you will have to attend.

- Does it fit in with your development plan and/or school priorities? If it does, ask yourself the following question. If not, then politely decline the offer. Your school cannot be allowed to become distracted from its priorities.

- Do you already have the expertise in school to deliver the support being offered? If so, then do it yourself. If not, consider the offer – but before doing so, ask yourself the next question.

- Does your school have the capacity (time and finances) at the moment to organise the logistics to take part in the event and keep disruption to a minimum when lessons are being covered? Is there an easier, cheaper and less disruptive way to take part? For example, sometimes it is easier for a whole year group to participate rather than part of a year.

- What are the outcomes? Will there be any measurable impact? If the answers to these questions are not clear, then ask the person making the request to clarify the rationale for the activity or request.

If only I could invent a scoring system which accurately weighed the advantages of participating in various events against the disadvantages of supply cover and staff not available for duty at break and lunch. I would make a fortune!

Being organised and systematic

Ask a member of your admin team to keep a log of the enrichment opportunities each year group has undertaken. Obviously, it is important to offer enrichment, especially if it enhances learning within specific subjects. However, too much of this and there is a danger of the curriculum not being delivered fully. Too many enrichment activities also runs the risk of certain students benefiting from them more than others, particularly if you don't keep a record of the events. And, don't forget, those left in school are likely to be the recipients of cover lessons.

Likewise, it is useful to keep a log of all the events that staff attend too. Without this, you may suddenly realise towards the end of the year that one or two members of staff have been off-site far more than the others. Consider the implications this will have for the classes they teach to help you decide whether or not particular activities should take place.

Finally, do you have a PA or senior team admin officer? If so, they will be (or should be) an integral element in the smooth running of the SLT. In small schools, it may be difficult to include a PA in your budget but in larger schools this role is essential. It is worth you both going through your mail and email together for a few weeks, so the PA can learn to identify the obvious things they can delete or respond to without bothering you first. If you share your mailbox with your PA this can greatly reduce your workload. We will return to this role and the make-up of the senior team in Cog 1.7.

Cog 1.6: Leading versus managing

Up until now, this chapter has focused primarily on the influence that a head has on the school and the leadership qualities they must show to ensure they consistently exude the positive ethos they want to see across the school – that is, leadership rather than management. The distinction between managers and leaders is worth exploring further if we are to ensure that leadership at all levels in a school is excellent.

The birth of leadership in schools

Much has been written about the differences between leaders and managers. Anyone in a leadership position has to do both, but what do these roles actually involve? In the nineties, the term 'leadership' really took off in schools. In a previous school, the senior management team (SMT) disappeared overnight and was replaced by the SLT. There was no real explanation and so, naturally, the staff mocked the term: 'Who do they think they are?' 'Are we supposed to bow when they pass?' 'Are we all sheep being led?' We thought it was just another passing fad among the millions of other fads we were being bombarded with at the time. It will pass, we thought, but it didn't.

After a term or two of the staff still referring to the senior team as the SMT, we had a training session on leadership. Here we learned that there were a lot of different types of leadership: instructional, transformational (these are discussed in more detail later in this cog), post-modern, participative, invitational, contingent, managerial, pedagogical. The list went on and on and it didn't help us very much. For me, school leadership suddenly seemed to be very complex. It took an MA and a recognised head teacher qualification before I really got to grips with it all and realised that my own prejudices and insecurities were making me ignore the sense in the name change. Meanwhile, as time went on, middle managers became middle leaders and heads of department became subject leaders.

The focus on developing school accountability led to a shift in thinking around school leadership. No longer was it enough to be the managerial head of a school, managing the day-by-day, year-by-year activities of staff, budgets and other administrative duties. Someone was now required to take control and lead the school forward on an ongoing journey of improvement.

It is worth mentioning that my initial cynicism about the term SLT was partly to do with my interpretation of the word leadership. I saw a leader as someone who led people on a leash, so to speak, and who people followed blindly. I didn't think about the word in its wider context. I was used to being told what to do or, as we referred to it, managed. I didn't regard the deputy at one school as being a good leader when he identified a fantastic work-related learning course for me to go on and encouraged me to follow this route. Nor the head of my next school who spotted me doing a presentation on work-related learning and asked if I had thought of applying for a role in her school. (She appointed me and gave me the autonomy to develop the role, while monitoring my progress closely.) In my eyes, at the time they were senior managers.

My prejudices also stemmed from the standards agenda that accompanied the drive for accountability at the time, which only muddied the waters when it came to defining leadership. Heads whose schools gained good GCSE results were automatically defined as good school leaders, as were those who parachuted into schools and instituted unsustainable resources and practices to achieve results quickly – and then were called 'super heads'. I am sure that many were good school leaders, but were also those who were in fact good school managers: good at managing an exam system which, at the time, could be manipulated to meet the prescribed standards.

As a head, or in any leadership position for that matter, you are not a leader because you manage things well; that is only a small part of the job. You are a leader because you have a vision and you can influence others to follow that vision. If you manage your school or your department towards achieving good results quickly, but you don't know how to take the department or school forward (i.e. no vision, no resource/capacity left to improve further, no willingness from the staff to support you), then you are not on track to becoming a good leader.

A leader should have a clear vision based on a consistent set of principles and the ability to influence others (we will examine this in more detail in Cog 2.2). These are, in my opinion, the two main ingredients of good leadership and go hand in hand. The types of leadership listed above are supported by different theories, but all leadership stems from vision and the ability to influence and bring about the change you want to see.

As school leaders, we often ask how or whether we should be managing our staff. I can barely manage my own children! As parents, we set times for our children to be home or give them tasks to do around the house. Sometimes it works but often this is only because there is the threat of something being withdrawn if the task isn't completed. Managing people doesn't give them the space to develop independently and grants them little sense of ownership or motivation to complete a task well. I am reminded of a quote by Grace Hopper (an early computer programmer and US Navy rear admiral): 'You manage things, you lead people.'[11] This really resonates with me.

You can easily manage things; things don't argue back, so you can organise and manipulate them without fear that they will say no. If others are involved with these things, you can influence or lead them to elicit their support. Management is often described as a science and leadership as an art. Devising a timetable is a skill that can be learned; there is a science to it. In other words, it is objective. You

---

11 Philip Schieber, 'The Wit and Wisdom of Grace Hopper', *OCLC Newsletter*, 167 (March/April 1987). Available at: http://www.cs.yale.edu/homes/tap/Files/hopper-wit.html.

can read up about it, learn how to do it and, hopefully, it should go according to plan.

It is the people involved in your timetabling that will make things messy, and this is where the art comes in. How we work with, influence, inform, coerce, motivate and inspire people will vary from individual to individual. It is a subjective beast rather than an exact discipline. The art is in being flexible, attentive, empathetic, reasonable and respectful – just some of the qualities that make a good leader. These characteristics can be learned over time through practice and experience. Your staff won't learn and develop these qualities if they are managed.

Consider the subject leaders and senior leaders you have worked with during your career. To what extent have you been given the autonomy to develop your practices and skills? Have you quickly picked up on any errors or flaws in your practice by noticing good modelling in action? Were you consequently inspired to work hard for the person leading you? If so, this was good leadership in action. Alternatively, have you been left to your own devices and given very little feedback, resulting in you adopting an initiative that didn't really fit with the vision or ethos of the school? This highlights how important it is that a leader has a clear and transparent vision, as well as the ability to influence others.

Possessing strong influencing qualities can also be detrimental to effective leadership, especially when you add ego to the equation. When I first embarked on developing project-based learning as a deputy in 2002, I was passionate about it and managed to encourage and inspire quite a few people to follow me. In truth, I don't think I had a clear enough vision: I was working through my ideas without knowing where it was going, which led to many U-turns and much confusion. However, people still believed in what I was doing, so I must have articulated the concept well and I am sure my position as deputy held some weight. In hindsight, I wasted people's time. This is the worst type of leadership. If applied to a whole school or MAT – where there are hundreds and possibly thousands of people involved – things can go spectacularly wrong.

If you take anything from this section, it is that you cannot lead on charisma or force of personality alone. Consider former politicians and world leaders – who has left a lasting legacy? We may remember those who were charismatic (in positive or negative ways), but those who have left a positive legacy have more than charisma. When walking into a difficult situation that needs to be repaired fast, it is easy to fall into a quick-fix trap. Leadership is not about arriving at a school, raising results and then leaving. Rather, it is about embedding sustainable practices and systems which help young people and staff to grow and flourish. That is what a good school leader should aim to achieve first and foremost, regardless of their role.

Transformational and instructional leadership

Before moving on, it is worth returning to two leadership models mentioned above: transformational and instructional. According to Ryan Shatzer's comparison of the two theories,[12] transformational leadership centres on:

- Developing and articulating a vision effectively.

- Bringing staff together and working towards common goals.

- Modelling the practices you want to see to ensure high expectations.

- Developing an environment that encourages professional self-reflection and intellectual stimulation, which leads to current practice being questioned, challenged and developed.

- Looking after the needs of staff to create an environment where people enjoy coming to work.

Instructional leadership focuses far more on:

- The head teacher developing, directing and supervising the curriculum and instruction in the classroom.

- A more hands-on approach with teachers in order to improve teaching and learning.

- Goal-oriented tasks.

- Establishing high expectations and standards for teachers and students.

---

12 Ryan H. Shatzer, 'A Comparison Study Between Instructional and Transformational Leadership Theories: Effects on Student Achievement and Teacher Job Satisfaction'. Dissertation, Brigham Young University (2009), pp. 15–30. Available at: https://scholarsarchive.byu.edu/etd/2432.

A review of successful school leadership by Christopher Day and Pamela Sammons found that the impact of instructional leadership (they refer to it as pedagogical leadership) 'is nearly four times as much as transformational leadership'.[13]

If you take a step back and reflect for a moment, you will notice the priority I have given to leading a school and instructional or pedagogical leadership. I haven't included a chapter in this book on curriculum models or teaching and learning, for example. That wasn't because I regard them as second division when it comes to school improvement; their development plays an equally important role. However, they go hand in hand with the more subjective aspects of ethos-driven school improvement.

The principles related to ethos in this book, which in the main describe aspects of transformational leadership, provide the foundations for good teaching and learning and pedagogy. Day and Sammons echo this in the following statement: 'In successful schools, headteachers were able to combine "collaborative capacity-building with a keen pedagogical focus". In short, they were found to exercise leadership that was both transformational and pedagogical in its focus.'[14]

I highlight these two models because it is important to hang on to the transformational aspect of school leadership, especially when a school does not have firm underpinning values and may be in difficult circumstances. This also applies to departments. Those who hold your school to account may encourage you to adopt a more instructional form of leadership, but I would argue that while this may lead to quick wins, they may not be sustainable, especially if the school has a poor ethos.

Management has its place – a model for staff development

In a school or department in very challenging circumstances, the leadership qualities of vision and influence are, as always, vital. You will also need to take the time

---

13 Christopher Day and Pamela Sammons, *Successful School Leadership* (Reading: Education Development Trust 2014), p. 22. Available at: https://www.educationdevelopmenttrust.com/EducationDevelopmentTrust/files/a3/a359e571-7033-41c7-8fe7-9ba60730082e.pdf.
14 Day and Sammons, *Successful School Leadership*, p. 22; citing Viviane Robinson, Margie Hohepa and Claire Lloyd, *School Leadership and Student Outcomes: Identifying What Works and Why. Best Evidence Syntheses Iteration (BES)* (New Zealand: Ministry of Education, 2009), p. 93. Available at: https://www.educationcounts.govt.nz/__data/assets/pdf_file/0015/60180/BES-Leadership-Web-updated-foreword-2015.pdf.

to assess the capability of your staff, and you may have to acknowledge that some individuals are not in a position to work autonomously.

One method I have adopted to develop staff illustrates effectively how transformational and instructional leadership working together can lead to sustainable practices at a pace which is appropriate to the needs of the school community. At Eastern High we used a graduated approach to staff development. The model was adapted from a pedagogical approach I had designed to develop independence in students. Teaching staff are taken through the following four stages:

- The first stage is *didactic*. This is necessary if you inherit a staff who have had no clear leadership, guidance or systems to follow. The same applies to young people who initially need to be told where, when, what and how. As you make your assessments on staff (or students), some or all can move on to the next stage.

- This second stage is a period of *testing and negotiation*. How much can you trust your staff (or students) to work independently? To what extent do they need guidance, interventions or restrictions?

- The third stage is reached when staff (or students) have reached a level of competence or *independence* such that they can be given *autonomy* (with continuing monitoring and some guidance) to carry out their roles or tasks and develop them further.

- The fourth stage continues with the same level of autonomy as in the third stage, but the member of staff (or student) has reached a stage where they can take on their own *leadership* roles and provide guidance and/or influence others.

This is a stepped model towards leadership: initially, there is a degree of management and the recipient is guided and coached towards the next stage. Solely trying to manage is not a growth model and is an easy trap to fall into.

This is echoed in four factors highlighted by Day and Sammons which determine how we distribute leadership:

- the headteacher's judgement of what is right for the school at different phases of its development
- the headteacher's judgement about the readiness and ability of staff to lead

- the extent to which trust has been established
- the headteacher's own training, experience and capabilities.[15]

The four-stage model I have described looks good on first reading and should work in theory, but this is where simple descriptions have their flaws. There is a veritable minefield of complexity underlying this strategy. When I use the model, I question myself continuously: do I tend towards managing and not letting go enough to allow staff to grow and develop? What will enable me to move from stage 2 to a more distributed leadership model at stage 3, and even more so at stage 4? We will explore the complexities of managing this process in Cogs 1.7 and 1.8.

Cog 1.7: Developing a team

Going into a school for the first time as a head and meeting your senior team is not easy. There are so many sensitivities. From your perspective, you are most likely hoping that you can work with the current team, that they are capable and that they will support you. From their angle, it will be more along the lines of: is my job safe? Is this person any good? What are his/her *real* plans?

It is true that heads tend to prefer to have their own teams around them – teams they have appointed. Before the rise of high-stakes accountability there was perhaps less senior leader movement between schools, but today it is a different story. The majority of senior staff understand that if their results have been continuously poor, and the school ethos likewise, then questions are going to be asked of the leadership team. Hence, it is much harder to go in and feel relaxed with the team you have inherited.

15 Day and Sammons, *Successful School Leadership*, p. 54.

In my first school as head teacher, as part of the transition process to academy status, a restructure at senior level had already been calendared in, so the strategy was fairly transparent. However, in my previous two positions, where both schools had been in the bottom 10 for results and exclusions in the country, no restructure was scheduled. In both cases, the senior teams looked at me with suspicion from the moment I stepped into the school. They knew I would want to get to know them for a short while and then announce a restructure. This is an unfortunate scenario: the quality of the leadership team is certainly one of the top factors that contributes to school improvement and, of course, a positive school ethos.

I have painted a rather ruthless picture in which heads come into failing schools and remove senior teams indiscriminately. The reality is most often not as grim. Although some form of restructuring is likely to be necessary (especially in a failing school), this does not automatically mean a loss of personnel. Teams are not only about personalities, which may change over time but are nevertheless fairly fixed. The attributes of effective teams also include skills and knowledge that can be learned and improved on. This is an important factor to bear in mind when considering the staff you have available and the type of team you want to build.

Re-examine your own strengths and the type of leader you want to be

When considering your ideal team, the first thing you need to consider is your own strengths and character. There is no point trying to replicate yourself on the team a half a dozen times, and it is certainly a bad idea to appoint the people you think you will get along with best – that just makes for more versions of you. For example, I am not a completer finisher.[16] I try to be, I really do, but I am easily distracted and always looking at the next thing (I have it under control these days – honest!). People with an attention to detail and who ensure every box is ticked may have a very different personality to me, and I may not naturally gravitate to them outside of a work environment, but they are an essential part of my team because they complement my strengths.

....

16 Dr Meredith Belbin identifies nine different team roles: resource investigator, teamworker and coordinator (social roles); plant, monitor evaluator and specialist (thinking roles); and shaper, implementer and completer finisher (action roles). For more information see Meredith Belbin, *Management Teams: Why They Succeed or Fail*, 3rd edn (Abingdon and New York: Routledge, 2010).

Don't forget that it is all about balance – for example:

- Some people have a natural charisma, lead exciting assemblies and inspire staff and parents, but you also need those who are more grounded and relate better on a one-to-one level and when dealing with more practical matters.

- You will need your ideas people but you also need those who will guide the team back to the priorities and plan (that should also apply to you as the head). These are the individuals who are close to headship themselves and can see the big picture.

- You may need the nurturing, caring kind who will champion the needs of students but you will also need to balance this with the functional person who will not be afraid to say, 'Hang on a minute, that child is costing the school £XXX in terms of support and time taken. It's not sustainable.'

- At times you need decision-makers who are confident enough to make decisions without always seeking everyone's approval but you also need the democrats who would prefer to consider the views of others as well.

Your job is to sit in the middle and listen to the different viewpoints and make the final decisions. Mixed teams make for more debate and argument, but this is healthier and can be far more productive in moving a school forward. Hopefully, you will recognise some of the traits mentioned above in the team you inherit; just don't forget the need for balance.

Don't write off the current team before you have met them

It is too easy to do: you look at the results, the past inspection reports and other data you have assembled, and already you will have formed opinions before you have even set foot in the school. On top of that, it might suit you to think that the whole team are underperforming because wouldn't it be easier to have a team you have appointed yourself and know you can trust?

Give them a chance! Restructures take time, so even if things seem bad on first impression, a brief delay won't slow down the process too much. Challenge your team with regard to all aspects of the school, but ensure they don't see this as a negative challenge. Ask them to carry out a review of the area of the school for which they are responsible. It is their chance to show you just how much of a grasp they have on the current situation and how effectively they are dealing with it.

For some staff members, a review of the area where they assess performance, including what is going well and some priorities for improvement, can be completed quickly. They will have the relevant information to hand and a firm grasp of the situation. Others may struggle to produce the data you require and may not have the leadership or management skills to implement an effective review. If you are taking on a successful school or replacing a head teacher who is moving on naturally (for promotion or retirement), this review will still be an important activity as it will give you clarity about your priorities. Most of the information you require should be available on the current school self-evaluation form (SEF), so hopefully your team will use this to pull together the data. You can also conduct some of your own verifications to establish what in the SEF is actually occurring on the ground.

The other reason for not being too hasty with any restructuring is that there may be some gems on the staff whom you may overlook. In all my schools, among the chaos of school closure or falling into special measures, there have always been some individuals, either on the senior team or one step away from it in a higher middle leader role, who are very capable, but in the wrong place at the wrong time. There are also the members of staff who have the ability, skills and knowledge, but who may have had poor role models and few opportunities to develop. These staff are well worth looking after and nurturing; this is transformational leadership in action.

Cog 1.8: Do you dare delegate?

If I were to draw out one point from the previous cog, it is that whether you are leading a team or a school, there is a real tension between leadership and management. The temptation is always to tend towards management because the buck stops with you when it comes to responsibility for the area or people you lead. You want it all to go well and so you may, unwittingly, slip into management mode and try to over-organise everyone and everything according to your (or your leader's) vision. Before you know it, practices become didactic and you lose the support or respect of those you lead.

Accountability and the weight of responsibility can make it difficult to delegate effectively, but you can't do it all. This is an obvious thing to say but we ignore the advice continually. For example, as a senior leader and deputy I always produced the timetable and I was responsible for the curriculum and teaching and learning. These areas of school leadership have always been dear to me, so I found it very hard to let go of them when I became head. I have done this little by little, and each time I have relinquished one of these areas I have seldom regretted it.

If delegation is going to be successful, there are a number of key factors to consider:

- Know your staff well. Is the person to whom you are delegating the area or task capable of fulfilling it?

- Will they need any support? If so, the person doing the delegating may need to take on a coaching or facilitation role. (I use these terms rather than line management because while there needs to be an element of monitoring progress and outcomes, as required by line management, there also needs to be support and guidance where necessary.)

- Be clear about your expectations for the task or responsibility.

- Be prepared for things not to be implemented exactly as you envisage it. We all interpret situations differently and work to our strengths; the outcomes may be better than your initial expectations.

- Using the word 'ownership' can be very effective. It helps to highlight the fact that the delegatee is fully responsible for the role or task and has a high degree of autonomy for taking it forward and developing it. I always include it in my improvement or development plans.

- Make sure you don't lose a sense of the bigger picture when delegating tasks downwards. Give people leadership of certain aspects of the whole vision by encouraging, influencing and coaching them to develop that area.

There are also pitfalls to avoid when delegating:

- Monitor the extent to which the tasks or responsibilities you have delegated are being re-delegated. I have known senior or middle leaders to be entrusted with a task, only for them to give it to someone else and leave them to it. Miscommunication can set in when this happens: there are misinterpretations and ideas are watered down. Not only does this worsen each time a task is delegated downwards, but it is also accompanied by a loss of drive and shrinking sense of ownership.

- It is a sign of poor and unethical leadership to throw someone in at the deep end or lay a trap for them. I have seen leaders question the capability of an individual and then delegate a task to them to prove it. Everyone needs the opportunity to develop. Intentionally setting someone up to fail will not only reflect badly on you but could also lead to a grievance procedure being taken out against you. If you are unhappy with the performance of a member of staff, there are better ways to address this, as we will touch on in Chapter 4.

- Be wary of the over-confident member of staff who tells you not to worry and they have it all in hand. I have fallen foul of this when being talked into passing over responsibility for aspects of the school by an assertive and articulate individual and then not providing sufficient monitoring or coaching. Some career-minded and driven members of staff can be very persuasive but do not have the leadership experience to take on big roles yet. Don't curb their enthusiasm, but assign them to more manageable roles within their current skill set.

- Be especially aware of the willing-to-please member of staff. Tasks and responsibilities should not be dumped on the most accommodating. There are people like this in every school, who end up with huge workloads because they don't like to say no or 'I have reached my capacity at the moment.' Protect these individuals and don't add to their burden.

If done well, delegation can contribute to a positive school ethos. It gives staff an air of collective responsibility, with everyone working to a common purpose and goal. It models good collaborative practice, which is what we should be aiming for in all our staff and students. It is harder for some school leaders to delegate than others, and therefore it is vital that you are honest about your own feelings when it comes to delegation. As we will explore in Chapter 4, delegation is a major factor when it comes to creating a sense of belonging for staff. Look for opportunities to delegate, then trust the person to carry out the task, but don't overlook the need for comprehensive monitoring and accountability systems.

What to take from this chapter

It is so easy to become overexcited and enthusiastic about your latest idea and rush into it, expecting all your staff to follow. Alarm bells should sound when the SLT latches on to a bright idea and jump straights into it without due attention being given to the road map, improvement plan or vision. Or, worse still, without examining where the staff body are in terms of their expertise, capabilities and capacity.

At Eastern High there was much to improve and put in place, but that was yet another trap waiting for me to fall into: trying to do everything at once. I was brimming with ideas from my last two headships and I was also under masses of pressure to make changes as quickly as possible. The road map described in Cog 1.4 was born of necessity; it was a way to keep myself and the senior team in check. It enabled us to develop the school in an orderly and manageable way and kept those to whom we were accountable at bay by showing them the school's capacity to improve and at what rate we could make progress. The stepped model of staff development, outlined in Cog 1.7, ensured that we made improvements in a measured and controlled way.

A school's ethos will be guided and established by the quality of its leadership team – that is, how well it knows its own capacity and capabilities as well as that of the school or departmental areas. A school that tries to emulate Icarus and does too much too soon will stumble and fall. Good leadership will set an achievable level and pace. More than that, good leadership will set out the strategy for realising that vision, which will further cement a school's ethos, as we will see in the next chapter.

Chapter 2

An Ethos of Vision, Purpose and Direction

You've got to think about big things while you're doing small things, so that all the small things go in the right direction.

Alvin Toffler[1]

The diagram on page 50 highlights the importance of having a vision underpinned by sound principles which guide everything you do in leading and managing a school or a specific aspect of it. Without a vision, effective leadership and sustainable school improvement is not possible. For me, this is the most important topic in this book, so forget any thoughts of, 'Oh, I'll come back to it later.' If you really want to know about the foundation and core of a school's ethos and school improvement, read this chapter.

The vision is the beating heart of the school, influencing every facet of school life and ensuring constancy of ethos throughout. Not one of the schools I have led would have achieved the same level of success had there not been a strong vision in place based on a secure set of related principles, values and beliefs. It sets a challenge for all of us, something to aim for. If the vision is owned by both staff and students, it can serve as a motivator, especially if progress towards it is jointly planned and monitored. I make no apologies for trying to oversell the importance of having a vision – if you get it right, your school or department will be transformed.

In this chapter, we will explore the development of an ethos of vision, purpose and direction in the following way:

● In Cogs 2.1–2.3, we introduce the concept of vision in schools and the importance of having a robust rationale which fortifies the vision and the

1   See https://tofflertrust.org/about.

Our principles

- This is what we believe education is about.
- These are my own 'rules'.
- They are based on a sound rationale.

Vision statement

- This is what the school will aim to achieve
- Every strategic decision we make and system we put in place will relate back to this.

Value/belief statements

- This is how our principles will manifest themselves in the school.
- We will work with stakeholders to develop these into statements of intent.

Policy, systems and processes

- Evaluation and planning of:
  - Leadership.
  - Pedagogy.
  - Curriculum.
  - Relationships.
  - Use of resources.
  - Environment.

context within which it sits. Exploring these cogs will better equip you to answer the following questions:

> To what extent should a school vision be a central feature of school improvement?

> How do we form a vision with a sound rationale which encourages others to believe in it and follow it?

> What is the purpose of schooling and how does this inform the rationale for a school vision?

- Cogs 2.4 and 2.5 focus on developing underpinning principles and the first steps to forming a vision. These cogs will help you to answer the following questions:

> What would be the vision for my school if I had my own way?

> What principles do I ascribe to with regard to education and schooling?

> How do we collectively form value statements which support our vision?

- Cogs 2.6–2.8 take us through the process of bringing the school vision to life, ensuring that it stays alive and constantly influences the direction and purpose of the school, as well as its systems, processes and practices. These cogs will enable you to answer the following questions:

> How can I make the vision easily accessible to every member of staff and ensure they know and understand the vision?

> How can I ensure that the vision informs planning and strategy?

> What checks are in place to ensure the school makes progress towards its vision and is not distracted by systems or activities which don't support or contradict the vision and the principles it upholds?

Cog 2.1: It's not just a vision statement, it's a way of life!

Vision or mission

Are all staff and students working towards the school's vision? This may seem an obvious question, but all too often a school will work hard to create a vision statement, pin it up around the school and highlight it in the prospectus, yet it may not be embedded in day-to-day attitudes and behaviours. Does it underpin everything you do in your school?

Before exploring these questions further let us consider the impact that a clear vision for your school ought to have (providing your staff and students have bought into it). The vision should:

- Form your ethos; it should be the heart and soul of the school.
- Support and strengthen your school ethos.
- Inform your curriculum.
- Help you to make strategic, long-term and day-to-day decisions.
- Form your code of conduct (for staff and students).
- Develop the pedagogical approach taken by the school.
- Guide your relationship with the community and partners.

In short, the school vision should enable the school to have a consistent focus, preventing it from flying off at tangents and never quite completing what it sets out to do.

It is important here to draw a distinction between a vision and a mission. Schools and companies often have a vision statement and/or a mission statement, and it can be easy to confuse the two. However, there is a very real difference, so it is important for the sake of clarity to make a distinction. I use the following definition in this chapter:

> A vision is your school's goal – where you hope to see it in the future. The mission provides an overview of the steps planned to achieve that future. A vision is concise and easy to recall, whereas a mission is lengthier and more explanatory in nature.[2]

To put this another way: vision statements concern themselves with the future of the school and its ultimate goal for the young people they serve, while mission statements focus on the steps to achieving this goal – how to realise the vision.

As a head teacher, I have always used the vision statement to describe our intent. Mission statements can be too prescriptive or detailed, so may miss the mark on the fluid nature of a school ethos. This is because an ethos is primarily a way of being and doing rather than something to be achieved. The ethos of a school evolves and fluctuates day to day; it is a living thing and therefore it needs guidance. Prescriptive and inflexible mission statements are more likely to direct rather than guide and may send the school down paths you didn't expect and distract you from your vision. Vision statements, on the other hand, reinforced by the principles you wish to uphold, guide the school on its journey and preserve its ethos.

Why have a vision statement?

I have been accused in the past (even before I was a head) of spending too much time on making sure the vision and underlying principles were right before springing into action. I make no apologies to those who have said to me something along the lines of, 'We've spent too much time talking about the philosophy – let's just get on and do it!' The vision gives us direction, purpose and motivation. Without

---

2 Ernest L. McClees Jr, 'School Mission Statements: A Look At Influencing Behaviour', *International Journal of Humanities and Social Science Review*, 2(1) (2016): 50–54 at 51. Available at: http://www.ijhssrnet.com/uploades/volumes/1598808998.pdf.

it, we are at sea with no collective sense of where we want to be and no compass to guide us there. It is all too easy for school leaders to sidestep vision and values. You can probably get away with it for a while, but it will invariably lead to questions regarding your ability to enhance the learning opportunities for the young people in your charge.

As a head teacher, your decisions will be constantly scrutinised, and the direction, methodology and practices the school adopts will be closely monitored. From government and inspecting bodies through to governors/directors, parents, staff and students, they will all look to you for answers if things are not moving according to plan or to the benchmarks of those who hold you to account. It is a very similar situation for middle leaders too. The most useful tool for leadership, therefore, is a clear vision supported by principles based on a sound rationale. This is the means to not only respond to any questions that arise but also to avoid questions arising in the first place. Strong principles, which lead to a well-defined vision, are vital in the development of a truly successful school.

Vision? Oh yes, we have a vision

It is all very well having a vision but it has to find its way into everything the school does. Every element – from your school improvement plan to your teaching and learning interventions, from the way you monitor progress to your behaviour policy – should be working towards realising your vision. It should become a way of life for the school, but it can be hard to achieve.

Let us say you have been appointed to your first headship or subject leader role and it is four weeks until you begin. After the initial excitement, the sleepless nights begin: will I make an impact? How will I go about making an impact? Will the staff respect me? Where will I start? The endless questions that run around your head may well lead to you launching the next stage of your career with some quick-win strategies that look and sound good and have a visible impact. As a result, the staff are supportive, the parents are behind you and the students seem to be on board. Now what?

There is no harm in this approach; after all, it is good to make an initial impact. However, if you go through the same process a second or third time, then you are in danger of moving a school or department from one initiative to the next – or, worse, having multiple initiatives running at the same time and consequently reducing the school's capacity to do anything really well. In addition, what are the implications of the initiatives you put in place (which may all stem from different principles)? Do they in fact conflict with each other? A clear vision and set of values can prevent this from happening.

The following table provides some examples of where I have seen such conflicts happening in a school:

Stated values or vision	Some likely positives	Possible conflicts
We will provide an inclusive education for all.	A push on differentiation in the classroom. Personalised pathways or interventions.	A focus on interventions for 'borderline' students. Setting classes (not necessarily a negative) but then allocating the top sets to the best teachers.
Prepare our students for the world of work.	Employers involved in some aspects of the curriculum. Careers talks/conferences. Project-based activities (less common).	Learning focused solely on knowledge acquisition and preparing for exams. A curriculum focused on subjects/topics that don't exist in working life.
Prepare our young people for life in the 21st century.	An emphasis on developing a wide range of ICT skills.	Mobile devices banned from the school. Little to encourage appropriate use of technology. Lessons led in a didactic way by teachers from the front.

Stated values or vision	Some likely positives	Possible conflicts
We offer restorative approaches to behavioural issues.	Restorative approaches used to resolve any breakdown in relationships.	A fixed-term exclusion policy which leads to multiple exclusions each week.

During my first year as a head, I began to realise that I was falling into the initiative trap described earlier. We were the first Building Schools for the Future school (a short-lived government-led initiative for funding and building new schools), and I was keen to impress the powers that be. I wanted to make an impact personally and show everyone what an amazing head I could be (the ego wasn't in check!). We had a vision for the school, which had been developed in consultation with staff and the governing body (we had an interim executive board at the time as the predecessor school was to close and reopen as an academy). The vision was as follows:

Our students will enjoy their journey through our academy, and in doing so become ready and equipped to face 21st-century challenges and to succeed in an ever-changing environment.

Our stated values, which underpinned this vision, were:

We believe:

- In effective communication.
- That learning should be character building, raise aspirations and, above all, be enjoyable.
- In the need for high-quality, relevant learning experiences.
- In responsible citizens who have the confidence to make a positive contribution to society, where everybody matters.

The vision on its own had high ideals, and the beliefs (if worded more clearly) could have made for an exciting, forward-thinking school. Instead, all these grandiose statements stayed firmly in the prospectus, on the website and on a few posters dotted around the school. In short, like many schools I have visited or worked in, they were written (a painstaking process), celebrated initially and then only occasionally glanced at in passing, mostly by parents and seldom by staff.

When you are up against targets and external pressure to improve rapidly, you may forget the clear vision and principles you had when you first applied for the post. You might have impressed everyone at interview with your vision. It sounded fantastic in theory, but things begin to look different when you are actually running a school. Six months on and where is that vision now?

This scenario may sound rather obvious, but it is an easy trap to fall into and I certainly fell into it. I launched a million initiatives (at least that is what it must have felt like to my colleagues) to ensure the school was seen as successful in the eyes of those that mattered to me at the time. Sadly, in order of importance these would have been the Academies Division (a subsection of the Department for Education at the time), Ofsted, the interim executive board, the press and parents. You might ask, what about the students? As a deputy, and for most of my career before this point, I really did champion the students. It was easier to do this without the burden of headship. Now, as a newly appointed head, the students were the last thing on my mind. I might as well have written the following vision statement and beliefs:

We want to achieve the highest results possible and have perfect behaviour in our school so that Ofsted and parents are impressed when they visit.

We believe:

- High attainment in GCSEs and A levels is the be-all and end-all.
- There is no excuse for bad behaviour; anything less than perfect will not be tolerated.
- In excluding students if they don't behave.
- That risk-taking is a ridiculous concept.
- That the education system developed in the 19th century is still totally relevant today.

Scrutinise the school you are currently working with or in. Ignore the eloquent statements of intent in the school literature or on the walls and have a close look at the day-to-day practices. What do the lessons look like? Are they learning sessions (as the school may like to call them) or are they good old traditional lessons, just like the ones you experienced as a child (and probably your parents and grandparents too)? How is poor behaviour dealt with? How frequently is Ofsted (or whatever inspection body you have) discussed? How often are GCSE or A level outcomes (or the equivalent) mentioned? Are students really being listened to? What follow-up is there to student voice sessions? The list goes on. Can you spot any conflicts or clashes, like the examples highlighted in the table earlier on in this cog? I guarantee that you will find some.

Realising a vision takes time and patience, which governments, local authorities and some school governors tend to have little of. People like to see action and results, to see things being done. The pressure to appease the masses may be subtle or impossible to ignore, but whatever form it takes it will never go away entirely. This is the real test of your leadership. How resolved are you to realise your vision? What measures are you prepared to put in place to ensure you are really moving towards it, and not just quick fixes that give the impression of positive momentum? You may be moving forwards, but if it is without direction and the courage to stick to your values and principles, will you ever arrive at the place you want to be? How will you find a balance between easy remedies and staying on course towards that vision? These are questions for you to explore personally, but hopefully as we progress through this chapter and examine some of the related issues, things will become clearer for you.

I cannot express how important it is that you take the time to investigate, develop and gain insight into the principles and values that you hold dear. In this way you will gain a clear and, more importantly, authentic vision for your school. Being in touch with your principles and values will help you to make decisions that are in keeping with your vision both strategically and on a day-to-day basis. They will become a tool for you to use and the bedrock of your leadership. As the Reverend Theodore Hesburgh observed, 'The very essence of leadership is that you have to have vision. It's got to be a vision you articulate clearly and forcefully on every occasion. You can't blow an uncertain trumpet.'[3]

....

3   Quoted in Philip V. Scarpino, 'Reverend Theodore Hesburgh Oral History Interview', *Tobias Leadership Center* (6 January 2009). Available at: https://tobiascenter.iu.edu/research/oral-history/audio-transcripts/hesburgh-theodore.html.

Cog 2.2: How to sell your vision – forming a rationale

Before you begin to rush out and wave your vision flag, proclaiming to one and the values that are held dear by the school or department, you need to consider other stakeholders. It is possible to write up the vision yourself, based on your own principles, but senior leaders are not working in isolation; buy-in and ownership are critical. And don't forget, you don't know everything.

It is preferable to involve staff, students and governors when devising a vision statement for your school or department. You may wish to debate each word with staff but it is often more practical to establish a well-thought-through set of value/belief statements collectively. These can then be used to write the final vision statement with your leadership team, which should reflect these values as succinctly as possible.

To ensure consensus, it is vital that immediate stakeholders feel involved, but this is where things can become difficult for three key reasons. Let us take a whole-school vision as an example.

1   *Getting your own way*

    If you are convinced that what you believe in is right, then you will no doubt want to communicate your own values, principles and beliefs to others. However, it is always preferable to allow staff and governors time to discuss, debate and come up with their own ideas. Your skill will be in using the outcomes of these discussions to present a clearly defined set of statements. Problems will arise if the statements are contradictory to your own. What if your ego blinds you to the positive elements of the proposals?

It is difficult to answer this question without sounding like a Machiavellian despot. After all, it is your school and your career stands or falls on the strength of these statements. I was faced with this dilemma at Eastern High. Over the years, I had developed a school vision that was an amalgamation of elements from my previous schools. Although these vision statements weren't created entirely by me, I believed in them. At Eastern High, I encouraged staff to come up with their own suggestions, although I steered and facilitated the discussion. It was a valuable process. I later blended their ideas with some of my own and presented them to the staff. Ultimately, the wording was different, but the meaning and values from my original statements were still there.

2   *Ensuring clarity*

Whether you have followed a discursive process with your staff or not, it is essential that you develop ways to express your principles clearly and in a way that encourages dialogue. People will look for cracks in your rationale, although that can sometimes be a good thing. If at this stage, following discussion with staff, you are having second thoughts about your principles, then it is important to explore this fully and, if necessary, reassess. If you are not clear from the start, some staff members may start having doubts about your ability to lead. It is vital to invest time in examining your principles the first time around.

3   *Don't be rushed*

Your staff will demand action. They won't want to spend too much time engaging in high-minded philosophical debate. They will want you to develop behaviour systems, design the curriculum and explore teaching and learning methodologies. Be strong: this is time well spent. Not only will the staff pressure you to move on quickly but you too will want to. Don't be rushed into coming out with pat statements without thinking them through, as you need to be prepared to hold to these principles and carry them into every aspect of the children's lives in your school. I do not intend to sound alarmist, but your principles and subsequent vision are the most useful tools you have in relation to school improvement, so they should be your number one priority.

If the statements and final vision are not in line with your personal principles, then you have a decision to make. Are you happy to go along with them (after all, you should have some clear statements), or do you need to go back and re-examine the areas you are uncomfortable with? This dilemma highlights the need for you to monitor the process throughout and challenge when your own principles are being questioned.

Cog 2.3: The purpose of schooling and education – a lesson on pragmatism

A useful first step to forming a vision might be to consider the real purpose of schooling and education. On balance, we don't want to be at loggerheads with our stakeholders by holding aloft a vision that contradicts their rationale for the school. This might seem obvious, but once our vision and the resulting strategies we set out to realise that vision come into play, we may find that not everyone has been upfront about what they want from the school. Some things have been left unsaid.

For example, the vision at Eastern High is as follows:

At Eastern High, we strive to ensure that every student who joins our learning community will enjoy the journey and leave at the end of their time with us with the knowledge, capabilities and wherewithal to flourish in life.

We will discuss later how we formed this vision and what underlies it, but for now it is enough to say that we explore every avenue and aim to do everything within our capacity to give our students the best education possible which will enable them to flourish.

One avenue we investigated a couple of years ago led to us having a brainwave. I had heard that some schools in China were allowing teachers time to assess students' work and give them feedback on the same day. The reason was that feedback was their major priority when it came to maintaining student progress. In their opinion, timely feedback was beneficial in ensuring that students fully understood the concepts they had been taught before moving on. At the same time, I was reading *Visible Learning for Teachers* by John Hattie,[4] which backed up much of what I felt about marking and assessment and inspired me to re-evaluate our school day.

Could we create a school day that would provide teachers with additional time to mark work and perhaps give students one-to-one or small group tutorials? This would enable us to engage students in feedback in a meaningful way and encourage them to see and use feedback as part of the learning process. It would also give the students an opportunity to feed back opinions about their learning and how they felt their teacher was performing. As a senior team, we discussed the notion exhaustively and came to the conclusion that it would be a good investment of time.

We estimated that if we cut subject time, then the time dedicated to feedback would more than make up for it. A very brief description of the ensuing plan was as follows:

- We worked out a timetable that allotted the same proportion of time to subjects. The key difference was that the main teaching part of the day stopped at 1pm.

- Following the lunch break, we proposed to run practical subjects (such as PE, art, music, drama and design technology lessons) each afternoon for all of Years 7 and 8 and for those following these subjects as options at Key Stage 4.

- We planned supervised sessions for Years 7 and 8, so they didn't have to go home early.

- For Year 9 upwards, if they were not taking any of the practical subjects, we planned to offer an online curriculum (mainly extended pieces of work to reinforce the work done in class) for two hours in the afternoon at home.

....

4   John Hattie, *Visible Learning for Teachers: Maximizing Impact on Learning* (Abingdon and New York: Routledge, 2011).

This would free up time for teachers to set up a tutorial programme, which would deliver personalised feedback to students on a rota basis. When not providing feedback, teachers would be given time for marking. We figured that we could do this on most days of the week until 4pm, taking directed time into account. We spoke with staff about the proposed plan and they were unanimously in favour. Everyone agreed that the personalised feedback time would be a win-win situation, with staff having less marking to do (because there would be more verbal feedback) and students receiving much needed meaningful and effective feedback to accelerate their progress (blended learning in action).

This happened in 2016, but after two years of discussion and planning we had all but given up on it. The main reason was lack of support from external stakeholders, whose primary objection was the fact that school would finish at 1pm for many students. Their key concerns were:

- Most parents are at work, so who would look after the students (even though we would provide supervised provision for Years 7 and 8)? They argued that parents would not be happy.

- Other local secondary and primary schools may be disrupted by our students hanging around outside their gates.

- It would look bad from a public relations perspective: 'You mean you would have students out on the streets from 1pm?'

This was a real opportunity to put into practice a 21st-century vision for learning which utilised independent online learning and freed up teachers to provide more intensive learning opportunities. It wasn't our ultimate vision for the school, which was to enable young people to flourish in life; however, it was an important element in realising our vision.

I have given over so much time to describing this example because I believe it highlights how important it is to understand various stakeholders' opinions when it comes to schooling and education. Consider the three bullet points above. From a parent's point of view, it would appear that the purpose of schooling is to provide a safe place where young people are looked after while they are at work. From a government or local authority perspective, it would seem to be about social control: young people need to be occupied in meaningful activities, otherwise they will cause a public nuisance. We know this isn't what parents, local education authorities or governments would ever state openly as the purpose of schooling;

however, I allowed these arguments to defeat us and resorted to compromise. (Compromise and pragmatism are recurring themes in this book and in the life of a school leader!)

If we were to ask parents what they actually thought about the purpose of schooling, the most likely answer would be something along the lines of: educating young people to provide them with the knowledge and skills to gain employment in later life. Dig a bit deeper and they would also mention the social and emotional skills they hope schools will help to develop in their students.

Governments have a different view on the purpose of schooling and education depending on how liberal, authoritarian, democratic or centrally controlled they are. For example, in 2015, the then schools minister, Nick Gibb, in a speech describing the purpose of education, cited three objectives: 'Education is the engine of our economy, it is the foundation of our culture, and it's an essential preparation for adult life.'[5] He then went on to elaborate on these three aspects of education. Nowhere does he mention that schools are also a crèche where young people are looked after (albeit in a meaningful way), thereby allowing their parents to go out to work and contribute to the economy.

In summary, when beginning to consider your vision you must ask yourself for whom you are designing the school. The purpose of schools should not be focused on satisfying society's needs at the cost of the individual, it certainly shouldn't be about fulfilling government targets and I would hope it is not about social control. It should be about the needs of the young people attending the school. Your task is to come as close to fulfilling these needs as you can, without being thrown unceremoniously out of your school and being branded (not with hot irons but probably on social media) as an idealistic dreamer.

You will have to get the balance right between pragmatism and compromise, and accept that yes, to an extent, schools must consider the wants of wider society. However, I firmly believe that if you meet the needs of the individual, they, in turn, will go on to look after society quite nicely.

---

5   Department for Education and Nick Gibb, 'The Purpose of Education' [transcript] (9 July 2015). Available at: https://www.gov.uk/government/speeches/the-purpose-of-education.

Cog 2.4: What do you believe in?

Now that you have had time to consider the wider purpose of schools, the next step in forming a vision is to focus on your own principles, values and beliefs. You need to know and fully understand what you can discuss, argue and present with passion and authenticity.

How principled are you?

Having principles means to hold on to something you truly believe in. It is a fundamental aspect of leadership. Having no hard and fast principles will result in a blowing-in-the-wind style of leadership, which will leave your colleagues directionless and following their own paths, which in turn will result in contradictory and conflicting messages to stakeholders. It is vital that you form your principles carefully, spend time exploring your own beliefs and values, and come to your own conclusions about the nature of education and schools.

Of course, having a strong set of principles is all very well, providing they are based on sound reasoning and are not founded on unethical beliefs or values that don't place the students first ('place the student first' is a principle in itself). You won't last long in post if this is the case. Unfortunately, you may last a lot longer in post if you don't hold strong principles and are easily swayed by others. But is this really what you want? And, ultimately, will this be good for the school, the students and the community the school serves? What will be your rationale for making decisions? How will you recognise and prevent the self-interestedness of others from taking precedence over the needs of the students?

How principled will you be? The decision is yours. You can choose to make your values explicit to all or you can hold on to them as a private set of rules. Whatever you choose, just make sure you have thought them through. In my personal experience, when I have felt confident about my beliefs it has worked. Conversely, when I have floundered, it can be directly related back to insecurity in my own beliefs or values.

How do we form our own set of principles, values and beliefs?

Before you begin to think about involving staff in considering the principles or values to which the school should ascribe, put aside all thoughts about achieving higher exam results, looking good for Ofsted and so on, and ask yourself some questions to tease out your own beliefs and values about education and life in general. For example:

- What do I value in life?

- What do I believe in when it comes to education?

- What qualities would I want my own child to leave school with?

- Where do my beliefs and values stand in relation to the wider world?

Another good place to start is to consider why you entered the teaching profession in the first place. Research suggests that most teachers go into the profession for intrinsic or altruistic reasons (i.e. for the love of their subject, to work with children or for the genuine desire to develop and educate young people).[6] Contrary to what I might have believed, extrinsic reasons – such as good holidays and pay – are not high on the list. The same paper also draws on research which claims that as teachers progress further in their career, extrinsic reasons for remaining in the profession begin to take over as they become more jaded by policy changes and difficult working conditions. When it comes to leadership positions in schools, I would argue the contrary: the higher we are promoted, the more of ourselves and our personal lives we invest in the schools and communities we work within.

---

6   Charleen Chiong, Loic Menzies and Meenakshi Parameshwaran analyse and review a broad range of research focusing on reasons for entering the teaching profession and reasons for leaving in: 'Why Do Long-Serving Teachers Stay in the Teaching Profession? Analysing the Motivations of Teachers with 10 or More Years' Experience in England', *British Educational Research Journal* 43(6) (2017): 1083–1110.

Consequently, we begin to look for ways to bring about genuine change and improvements to the system. At least, that is the path we ought to follow.

In hindsight, I have enjoyed working with children, but I never felt it was my vocation in life. Having said that, with each passing year, I have become more determined to improve the life chances of young people. This is because, having given so much time to the profession and having become so frustrated by the policies and political manoeuvrings that prevent us from meeting the needs of all young people, I have begun to realise that I want to make a difference. Coming to this conclusion has certainly helped me in terms of recognising my own values. We all have different reasons for working in education but, hopefully, by the time we are ready to become a head of department or head teacher, most of us will be able to identify some concrete intrinsic or altruistic reasons for wanting to remain in the profession and lead a school.

Now that I have explored my own thoughts fully, I know that I am in the job because I want my students to leave school with the knowledge, skills, competencies and wherewithal to flourish in their lives. It is a big ideal but one worth aiming for. Some may argue that equipping young people with everything necessary to flourish in life is beyond the remit of a school, but I would contend that it is a worthy vision. The closer we come to all our students being able to thrive in the future, the closer we come to meeting what governments, local communities, parents and other stakeholders want of schools, but most importantly we make the needs of the young person our priority. We might not achieve our vision, because there are many external factors influencing young people's lives, but we can certainly aim to achieve it.

Underpinning the school vision are the principles and beliefs you hold dear to you. Your role is to develop these with your staff into value statements that establish a basis for the school vision and provide the core principles that will go on to form the school ethos. The ethos manifests itself in a consistent set of values and how the school lives and breathes this on a day-to-day basis. The next cog focuses on how these statements can begin to form the ethos of the school.

Cog 2.5: Blue-sky thinking – forming value statements

There is a strong element of blue-sky thinking when it comes to forming your value statements. They will be the backbone of your school, so they shouldn't succumb to compromise or be watered down to please stakeholders. Don't be afraid to be idealistic when it comes to sharing your most ambitious ideas.

To illustrate the process of developing clear value statements, I will describe the thought processes I initially followed and then proceeded to work through with staff and governors. This process helped us to establish our values and form a clear rationale for our vision. This led to a consistent ethos across all aspects of the school, which are encapsulated in the six statements on page 70. You may not agree with them, but nevertheless they serve as an illustration of the type of statements that can underpin a school vision. They also provide an insight into some aspects of schooling that I believe are imperative for the 21st century.

As we have seen, we wanted young people to flourish both in school and in their later lives. Our staff and governors agreed that this was a worthy aim for the school. However, it was important to say what this meant on a day-to-day basis – our mission. Furthermore, before we reached this conclusion, we had to unpick what our vision really meant. This required us to explore beliefs, principles and values which were common to us all and which explained why we felt the vision was important to us. In other words, what were the common building blocks for developing our school?

We carried out a number of mind-mapping exercises which explored all aspects of the school, such as curriculum, teaching and learning, student approaches to learning, and the local and wider community. We also framed our discussions within a context that featured current social and employment trends locally and globally to ensure that we considered the nature of the world our students would enter. Our reasoning took us along the following route.

● Firstly, we wanted our school to be community focused and an environment where young people wanted to attend daily, not because they were forced to by law but because the school belonged to them and played a meaningful part in their lives.

● Next, we explored what might put a young person off coming to school. Initially, we discussed the tension between staff and student when a student did something wrong or was being asked to do something they didn't particularly want to do. Through further discussion we acknowledged that young people are still developing and therefore will make mistakes, and that it was important that we accept this fact.

● This led us to think about all the different aspects of a young person's development – for example, controlling emotions, time management and managing relationships. We reasoned that if we wanted to enable our students to flourish, then as a school we should be focusing on all aspects of their development, not just literacy or numeracy. While we recognised that we did try to develop these other developmental aspects, we tended to deliver them in a tick-box way. For example, we taught students about time management in personal and social education lessons and then assumed we had covered it. Instead, we had to work out ways to give parity to all aspects of a child's development.

● We then wondered how we would ever find the time in the curriculum to teach all of these aspects, which, in turn, led us to call into question the word 'teach'. At this point, I recalled a presentation I had seen by Bob Pearlman, an educationalist from the United States, in which he stated that teachers no longer have a monopoly on information.[7] It had inspired me to think differently about the nature of our profession and the curriculum we offer. A deep understanding of pedagogy is what gives teaching its professional status, not our mastery of subject knowledge. There is a place for teachers to focus on difficult concepts within their subject areas (when we become the 'sage on the stage'); however, we have a more important

---

7   Bob Pearlman, 'Elements of Transformation: Transforming Secondary Schools for the 21st Century' [PowerPoint] (12 November 2004). Available at: http://www.bobpearlman.org/Kent.htm.

responsibility to use our pedagogical expertise to enable students to learn effectively in a more independent and/or collaborative way. This would free up time to focus on all aspects of a child's development.

- Next, we began to consider how teachers could work together to achieve this and the nature of learning sessions (as opposed to lessons). Could we work more collaboratively not only in our planning but also in our delivery? Could the students work more collaboratively, thereby learning from each other and developing the dispositions necessary to work with others effectively?

- During our discussions, we kept coming back to the role of technology and the way it was transforming all aspects of our lives. We were aware of its benefits but also acutely aware of its negative impact, such as cyberbullying, social alienation and the proliferation of fake news and disinformation.

- Finally, we needed to ensure that everything we did with our students was sustainable. There was no point in throwing everything at a few initiatives which would exhaust both the staff body and our budget. This was a long-term vision and required long-term practices (we will look at these in more detail in the next cog).

Don't get me wrong: this didn't take place in the neat way I have described. As well as structured meetings and staff INSET sessions, the process itself was long and drawn-out. It also included messy unstructured meetings, ad hoc conversations in the corridor with different members of staff and arguments within the senior team.

Eventually, we honed our ideas to six value statements. These expressed what we would be doing in school (our behaviours) to enable us to progress towards our 'flourish in life' vision:

1   We create a sense of belonging for all our students.

2   We accept that young people are still developing and will make errors of judgement.

3   We give parity to all aspects of a child's development.

4   A teacher's expertise lies in their understanding and mastery of pedagogy.

5   Information and communications technology is transforming the world, so we must learn to use it appropriately and safely.

6   Everything we do in school will have sustainability at its core.

On first reading, these statements may seem straightforward and manageable for schools to implement. However, once you begin to explore the implications of each one fully, it soon becomes clear that they demand a shift away from our current model of education (what Sir Ken Robinson refers to as a 'manufacturing model'[8]) and towards one which is conducive to nurturing the whole child.

These statements would bring the whole school together under one collective, consistent ethos. For example, by following the same set of principles for behaviour management, curriculum and pedagogy, we could avoid a situation where there might be an amazing 21st-century curriculum supported by a set of liberal principles, while at the same time behaviour practices that instilled a Victorian ethos (e.g. lessons behind closed doors, desks in rows, sanctions unrelated to learning).

We could have included a statement such as, 'All our lessons will be challenging and engaging.' However, assertions like these only cover one aspect of teaching and learning and could result in the school developing too many objectives. Instead, these six statements are close to first principles for our school. They are the roots of an imaginary tree, with the vision as the trunk. They don't specify specific practices; rather, they are values and principles that we, as a school, keep in mind when developing our practices.

---

8   Ken Robinson, 'RSA Animate: Changing Education Paradigms' [video] (14 October 2010). Available at: https://www.youtube.com/watch?v=zDZFcDGpL4U&t=144s.

Cog 2.6: Making it real – developing a framework

Whatever statements your school adopts, they will need to sit within a framework that will enable you to be strategic in your journey towards your vision. How will you evaluate progress? How do you plan to develop and improve further? A framework can also help to organise the practices, processes and systems you will adopt, making it easier to delegate and give ownership to particular people.

There is an element of choice here about how much of the wording and content of the value statements that underlie your school you incorporate into your framework. If we take as an example the six statements in Cog 2.5, some of these are very subjective. They set the tone for life in the school – the ethos. They are behaviours that pervade everything we do rather than actual practices that have measurable outcomes. In short, it could get messy if we tried to fit these into a framework for measuring the school's progress.

Although it is vital that our principles and values are not overly swayed by inspection frameworks, it is a fact that we live in a culture with strong accountability. If we drift too far from this baseline, it can become confusing and difficult to assess our development against other schools. Pragmatism again!

In the UK, schools are inspected regularly using various inspection frameworks depending on where they are located (see the table on page 73). The values that underlie your school may not fit comfortably into these formal frameworks, but there will be the need for a structure that links your school values to the standards expected of all schools. This is not only to appease inspectors but because it is right and proper that we do the best for our students, who will be measured against the performance of other students and who have a right to be cared for as well as any other child in any other school.

The following table shows the inspection areas for each of the four nations in the UK.

Inspection frameworks across the UK			
England (Ofsted) (2021)[9]	**Scotland** (Education Scotland) (2015)[10]	**Wales** (Estyn) (2020)[11]	**Northern Ireland** (Education and Training Inspectorate) (2017)[12]
Quality of education	Successes and achievements	Standards	Outcomes for learners
	Learning provision – quality of learning	Teaching and learning experiences	Quality of provision
Behaviour and attitudes	Learning provision – quality of care	Well-being and attitudes to learning	Care and welfare
		Care, support and guidance	Safeguarding

9 Ofsted, *Education Inspection Framework* (updated 23 July 2021). Available at: https://www.gov.uk/government/publications/education-inspection-framework/education-inspection-framework.

10 Education Scotland, *How Good Is Our School?*, 4th edn (2015). Available at: https://education.gov.scot/improvement/Documents/Frameworks_SelfEvaluation/FRWK2_NIHeditHGIOS/FRWK2_HGIOS4.pdf.

11 Estyn, *The Annual Report of Her Majesty's Chief Inspector of Education and Training in Wales 2018–2019* (2020). Available at: https://www.estyn.gov.wales/sites/www.estyn.gov.wales/files/2020-07/Annual_Report_2018_2019_en_2.pdf.

12 Education and Training Inspectorate, *Effective Practice and Self-Evaluation Questions for Post-Primary* (2017). Available at: https://www.etini.gov.uk/sites/etini.gov.uk/files/publications/isef-post-primary-with-shared-ed.pdf.

Inspection frameworks across the UK			
Leadership and management	Leadership and management	Leadership and management	Leadership and management
Personal development			Governance

The inspection areas in each nation are broadly similar and over the years have seldom strayed far from four main categories:

1   The quality of learning provision and outcomes.

2   Well-being, welfare and attitudes to behaviour.

3   Leadership.

4   Developing resources and the environment (this is admittedly a vague description, but one that we have adopted).

At Eastern High, we believed that our final value statement – the concept of sustainability – should be central to all we did as a school. In the same way as we had worked on our values, we unpicked what we meant by sustainability. We spent much time examining the needs of young people in the 21st century and continually returned to the four areas listed above, examining the extent to which they could meet the needs of our students.

We aimed to create a framework that would not only consider the sustainable practices we hoped to develop in our students, but also to look at the sustainable practices we would develop as an institution. The four key areas of sustainability we came up with were:

1   Sustainable, effective and meaningful approaches to learning.

2   Sustainable relationships and partnerships.

3   Sustainable mind, body and soul.

4   Sustainable use of resources and the environment.

This concept was relatively easy to understand and remember and could be easily developed into a framework to guide our evaluations, planning and practices. The framework would uphold all of our values, principles and beliefs and would be central to producing a curriculum, pedagogy and ethos that were consistent across the school. When establishing these areas of sustainability, we took into consideration two core issues: (1) the needs of the students now and in their future lives, and (2) our own practices, structures and culture. You will notice that these four areas closely match the inspection-related areas outlined in the table on page 73. Incidentally, the 'mind, body and soul' focus encompasses physical and mental health; the soul element is related to, among other things, aspirations and leadership.

When considering each sustainability statement, the SLT loosely followed Simon Sinek's notion of the why, the how and the what in order to explore the rationale (or why) for each statement, how we would achieve this in the school and what the impact would be.[13] As a consequence, we formed a five-year plan for the school which we have remained true to ever since.

Here is an example of one area of sustainability in our five-year plan:

Sustainable, effective and meaningful learning
Why develop sustainable, effective and meaningful learning?
Qualifications are valued – they are a passport for our future lives. However, to thrive in life and have the capacity to successfully meet the challenges of an uncertain future, we need to develop habits of mind and capacities to maintain growth. Learning should never end.
How will we achieve this?
• Through intensive coaching and mentoring of all our staff. • The application of a shared structure for learning which is consistent, collaborative and effective. • A curriculum focused on the development of literacy and numeracy and good habits of learning.

---

13 Simon Sinek, *Start with Why: How Great Leaders Inspire Everyone to Take Action* (New York: Penguin, 2009).

- Our curriculum offer is personalised for engagement, pace and challenge.
- All of our interactions will model, highlight and reinforce resilience, reciprocity, reflectiveness and resourcefulness.

What are our desired outcomes?

Students who:

- Meet or exceed their expectations in national performance measures.
- Are hard-working and resilient when meeting challenges.
- Can manage distractions and their time effectively.
- Understand the importance of learning and who develop a thirst for lifelong learning.
- Know what they can do to improve.

Staff who:

- Provide effective, meaningful and enjoyable learning experiences on a daily basis.
- Consistently provide challenge for students which encourages them to achieve their very best.
- Ensure there is relevance in their subject to real-world situations.
- Not only have excellent subject knowledge but are outstanding facilitators of learning.

A school that:

- Will develop and provide opportunities which will equip students with the knowledge, skills and dispositions to become effective and successful learners.
- Provides a broad curriculum which enables the identification of and focus on interests and talents.
- Ensures national priorities regarding teaching and the curriculum are fully addressed.

It is essential that you form a framework to plan, monitor and evaluate your progress. Your value statements can be used as headings, but if they are too narrow or too subjective you may wish to devise new headings which encompass all of your values. Don't forget that although you may have very high ideals for your students, you have to bring them sufficiently down to earth so they align with whatever accountability system you have to follow. Your framework doesn't have to replicate the inspection criteria exactly, but it does need to be easily assessed against national expectations.

To sum up this cog, developing a framework which encapsulates the vision for the school can be summarised as follows: begin with the end in mind.[14] In short, we need to know what we are aiming for before we set any wheels in motion. This will serve to draw out how the school will look and feel on a day-to-day basis.

Cog 2.7: Making it real – planning and strategy

The next stage is to write the school improvement or development plan (whatever you decide to call it). I don't have any perfect ways to do this, and I don't think there is any perfect model for a development plan. There have been many times in my career, whether as a head of department or as a member of the SLT, when I have questioned the point in writing one. 'Once it's done, we never look at it' is what I used to say and heard countless others say too. However, my opinion has since changed, and I can now definitely see the point of having a school improvement plan. Here are a few reasons.

---

14 I have borrowed this expression from Stephen R. Covey's *The 7 Habits of Highly Effective People: Powerful Lessons in Personal Change* (New York: Free Press, 1989).

The process is valuable in itself

The process of working on a plan – whether that is with your team or by yourself – focuses the mind. It will help you as a leader to understand where your priorities lie and to explore fully the priorities of your team and/or the school. Allowing others to write aspects of the plan and bringing the different areas back together for discussion or practical criticism can be an intense but valuable experience. It will develop not only individuals within the team, but it will also enable you all to take a step closer to being a highly functioning team. At the end of this undertaking, everyone knows what they have to do and all that is left to do is devise a review process.

Place a high importance on reviewing progress towards realising the goals of the improvement plan. I may be wrong, but I am sure that most of us don't religiously consult the plan until the day before we are due to evaluate progress in a particular area. This is the reason why we need regular, formal and collective reviews. Having said this, providing we ensure that we spend time discussing and exploring personal milestones and actions during the initial planning process, in my experience it is rare for an individual or team to not be on track.

It provides a rationale for others

Unfortunately, many people who will hold you to account have their own preconceived ideas about what an improvement plan should look like and what it should involve, to the extent that it becomes an accountability measure in itself. This can be off-putting when it comes to writing a plan. I have often asked myself what right someone else has to tell me how to present our plan or, worse still, what it should include. After all, it is our plan which will guide us on running the school and identifying its priorities.

Nevertheless, we have to accept that an improvement plan should be easily understood by others. As with your vision, it should provide a basis for what you are doing in the school, and if publicised well (e.g. summary posters), it constantly reminds staff of key issues for the year.

It prevents initiative-hopping

Underperforming schools and those schools in challenging circumstances all too often fall into the trap of jumping on the latest ideas that come along. MATs and local authorities regularly develop or endorse initiatives and encourage all schools to sign up to them. Even small events, such as a Year 10 Employer Day, held centrally, can use up much needed capacity in the school and detract you from your improvement plan. Even worse, it can prevent you from achieving certain goals in the plan.

A tight and transparent improvement plan can protect you from this dilemma. If you ensure that the plan is endorsed by your governing board and you regularly review progress against milestones with your chair of governors or executive head, it will give you a genuine reason – and evidence – to decline any offer that doesn't suit the school at that time. Conversely, it is important that your school doesn't miss out on beneficial initiatives just because they aren't in the plan; it is prudent to be flexible during the school year.

It protects you

If your improvement plan is tightly written and is endorsed by your governors or MAT, then those who hold you to account can't expect more of you. This is not an excuse to set yourself low targets. It is vital that team members are as realistic as possible when devising a plan and that it is made very clear to governors why the content of the plan is reasonable for the year. If progress is reviewed regularly, there will be no surprises if things don't go according to plan (which can happen all too easily in schools, given the number of variables).

The more those who hold the school to account are clear about the plan and the progress you are making with it, the better. If for some reason the plan is not on track, then everyone who has a stake needs to know and either offer support or extra capacity or agree alterations to the plan.

For example, if you know that your current cohort are going to have a set of results lower than the previous year, it is advisable to inform those who hold the school to account without delay. If the interventions you propose to make are backed up in the plan and/or you can show that you are acting on proposals in the plan, then governors, local authorities and MATs should be adding either their advice or their support. The point is: no one will be blaming the head or SLT if you have been open and transparent and agreed a set of intervention measures. You may know that the results won't match those of the previous year but, more importantly, you will also know that you have done everything within your capacity to maximise those results.

How should the plan be presented?

This is not an easy question to answer because there are many different ways to organise a school improvement plan. It is easy to fall into the trap of using a format that doesn't suit your school's particular needs but instead pleases certain stakeholders. Inspectors claim they don't mind how an improvement plan is written, but woe betide you if you don't specify impact precisely and objectively. Some governors want a plan with hundreds of columns with certain headings that you know you will never look at, while others want it to be so simple that it is ineffectual.

Rather than be specific, let us consider some key aspects that a school improvement plan should contain. Firstly, what period of time do you want the plan to cover? Our school has a road map which covers a period of around five years and specifies the headline areas we will address. We also have a five-year plan, which I find more useful than a one-year plan, as it gives us a realistic time frame to develop, implement and embed new practice.

What follows are some of the factors you should take into account when developing an improvement plan.

Be clear and concise about the areas on which you intend to focus

As we have seen, so much in relation to systems and processes in schools resembles a tree. I use my four areas of sustainability (the branches) as a framework for any plan we produce. As we extend into the smaller stems and twigs, each branch leads to more detailed elements, as in the following example.

Sustainable, effective and meaningful learning can be broken down into areas such as:

> Teaching and learning.

> Skill development (literacy, numeracy, ICT).

> Curriculum offer.

> Developing habits of learning.

Teaching and learning can be broken down into areas such as:

> Pedagogical practice.

> Monitoring practice.

> Coaching.

> Assessment for learning.

> Professional development.

Pedagogical practice can be broken down into:

> Challenge and engagement.

> Modelling.

> Collaborative learning.

> Questioning.

If we consider the branches above, the top level (sustainable, effective and meaningful learning) would be relevant in a long-term five-year plan where you perhaps develop different elements each year. The second level (teaching and learning) is similar; it is too broad an area for a one-year plan, unless you believe you have the necessary capacity in your school to address (from the example above) pedagogical practice, monitoring practice and so on. The third level (pedagogical practice) is a more realistic topic for a one-year plan, but even this may be too wide, especially if you have multiple sites (as Eastern High does). If so, my advice would be to focus on one or two areas, such as (again from the example above) challenge and engagement and/or modelling. In short, break your plan down into easily manageable chunks. I like to give responsibility for certain areas of the plan to members of my team, who in turn can identify more detailed areas to focus on and assign responsibilities for particular tasks.

Limit how much goes into the publicly available plan

Breaking down all the relevant areas into specific tasks and listing them all on your school improvement plan can lead to an overcomplicated and hard-to-read document; the salient points can become lost. I usually try to keep the fine details separate and ask the senior team to create their own Gantt charts for monitoring the completion of tasks.[15] In this way, we have a simple and accessible executive copy of the improvement plan. The individual Gantt charts can be shared with whomever would like to read them, as well as for review purposes by the SLT and, if necessary, in governor subcommittee meetings.

Be clear about the rationale for each task or activity and its intended impact

Some inspectors expect every item on the improvement plan for objective, measurable outcomes. Sometimes it comes down to semantics – perhaps we haven't worded something in an explicit way (e.g. we have missed out the word 'all'). As soon as you include percentages, you will be asked how you will measure them. However, just how do you measure the level of challenge in a classroom effectively, for instance? We get around this by having universal targets at the beginning of the plan, such as the percentage of 'good' and 'better' teaching and learning. We then signpost the contribution that a specific task or area of improvement will make to these whole-school targets. Another way is to use the terminology that inspectors employ rather than precise percentages (e.g. most, some, nearly all).

Highlight the costs and resources required

It is worth developing an improvement plan to coincide with your budgeting cycle because a really good plan will help to inform aspects of your budget. For this reason, aim to cost initiatives as accurately as possible in order to avoid unforeseen surprises that you can't afford.

---

15 A Gantt chart is a type of bar chart which breaks down the scheduled stages of a plan or project into specific activities with predefined start and finish dates.

An alternative model

I have become a bit braver recently and gone for a completely different model of planning. I still use a five-year plan, but for our annual plan for the school, I have been inspired by Amazon's founder and CEO, Jeff Bezos.

Jeff Bezos decided to remove PowerPoints from his meetings and replace them with narrative. Those presenting at meetings give everyone present a narrative to read in silence and then they discuss it. In his 2017 annual letter to shareholders, Bezos outlines his reasons for this shift, which were summarised and further explored by Carmine Gallo. In short: 'our brains are hardwired for narrative', 'stories are persuasive' and 'bullet points are the least effective way to spread ideas'.[16]

With Bezos' thoughts in our minds, we decided on what aspects of the school we wanted to improve over the coming year under our four areas of sustainability. Rather than filling in the usual tables, which always ends up feeling rather dry and pointless, I instead asked the team to go off and write a story for each area for which they were responsible. I wanted them to describe the school journey throughout the year as the developments were implemented and embedded. For example, how did people react? What difficulties did they face? What resources did they need? What was involved? What training was required? What were the outcomes?

My team looked at me as if I had finally lost my mind, but when I took out a story I had already prepared and asked them to read it (I was trying to be a good leader by modelling), they began to realise I was serious. So, we all went off to write our stories. When we reconvened to share them a few weeks later, we all felt the same. Not only had we all enjoyed the process, but we were also able to visualise the areas for which we were responsible and felt much clearer about the path ahead. Furthermore, the whole team understood fully what each of us was going to be working on. There was common purpose and real understanding in relation to the work each member of the team planned to do – something I had been trying to achieve for a number years without success.

---

16 Carmine Gallo, 'Jeff Bezos Banned PowerPoint in Meetings. His Replacement is Brilliant', *Inc.* (25 April 2018). Available at: https://www.inc.com/carmine-gallo/jeff-bezos-bans-powerpoint-in-meetings-his-replacement-is-brilliant.html. Bezos' original letter can be found at: https://www.aboutamazon.com/news/company-news/2017-letter-to-shareholders.

Our improvement plan is now a front-page summary listing our targets and key areas for development, followed by a number of stories which we try to keep to one page each. To satisfy inspectors and the like, we highlight actions and outcomes in two different colours. (This actually detracts from the narrative but it made some people happy.) The staff all have a copy of the plan and there have been positive comments across the board. Most of all, everyone likes how transparent it is. There are still Gantt charts for the SLT to follow but the stories are the central focus.

Cog 2.8: Making it real – ensuring the school is on track

Your quality assurance processes, performance reviews and school improvement plan should all inform the extent to which you are working towards your vision – providing they all relate back to and tie in directly with your vision statement and your set of belief or value statements.

We use inspection criteria to help us make this happen. I have no issue with this: inspection frameworks highlight areas of expected good practice. Furthermore, they don't interfere with the philosophy or vision of the school.

For each area of sustainability, we monitor our progress against the inspection framework using the following diagram. We map out the key inspection criteria for each sustainability and summarise them as one- or two-word descriptions. We then use presentation software to add the summaries to boxes which can be moved around within the diagram. We then spend an away day or a couple of evenings as a senior team deciding where each box should be positioned. On page 85 is an example populated with a few of the descriptions we use.

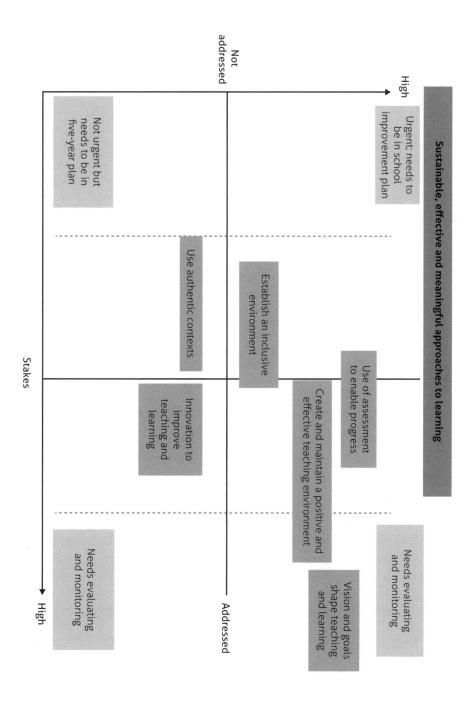

Members of the SLT who are responsible for specific areas may also have evidence to back up any assertions they make. Making copies of this diagram periodically throughout the year after each review is an excellent and quick way to illustrate progress.

Monitoring school processes

While this method of self-review is good for top-level discussions (we also use a similar model in departments), whole-school processes are essential if monitoring and evaluation is to be rigorous and effective.

What processes are we talking about? I am not a naturally organised person, but I have learned to use systems to help me be more efficient. Monitoring and reviewing progress is one of the aspects of a school that most needs processes in place to ensure that it happens successfully. The way we monitor progress with regard to whole-school self-review is as follows:

- There is a whole-school self-review document which is updated regularly on a four-week cycle. Every department follows this process and keeps their own review documentation.

- There is a timetable for the year to guide departments about which aspects of the school improvement cycle should be discussed at specific times of year.

- There are the usual SLT/head of department/line management meetings, with each member of the SLT responsible for certain departments.

- Each member of the SLT (including myself) is responsible for specific areas of our whole-school self-review.

- On a four-week cycle, a member of the SLT will meet with the head of every department (it is impractical to manage this on a shorter time frame) to go through aspects of the school improvement cycle for which they are responsible. For example, an assistant head may meet all of the department heads individually to discuss marking and progress in books.

- At the end of this sequence, each member of the SLT presents their findings from each area to the rest of the team. The outcomes from this meeting will be written into our self-review document.

- Intervening SLT meetings are scheduled to review other aspects of the school (e.g. book scrutiny) and progress towards meeting the aims of the improvement plan.

All aspects of review are scheduled into a calendar (we use Google Docs) and shared with all staff. There are also links in the calendar to meeting minutes in order to keep everything transparent. This transparency has also served to gain the trust of our staff and has certainly contributed towards a trusting collegiate ethos among staff.

What to take from this chapter

A school must have a vision – something to aim for and a direction of travel – with firm roots in the guise of a collection of agreed principles or values. If you want to create a strong and positive school ethos, it is paramount that this vision flows through every aspect of the school in a consistent way. Get it right and your vision will be your guide and reference point when things are difficult or tough decisions need to be made.

Develop the vision with your staff, students, governors and parents (through a parent forum), exploring the nature and purpose of education and schooling. Agree commonly shared values for schooling and education and work these into principles.

Create clear mission statements based on these principles, which will describe how the school will achieve its vision, and develop a realistic road map to get you there. Take into account that at times a certain degree of pragmatism will be required when working towards your vision, especially with regard to those who hold you to account. Having said that, a clear rationale (your principles and vision) will always hold you in good stead when it comes to explaining or justifying your reasons for doing things in a particular way.

Draw up a framework based on the values and principles that underpin your vision and mission statements. Ensure this framework is used in all planning, monitoring, review and evaluation. In turn, this will ensure that the vision is firmly embedded into all systems and practices throughout the school.

Finally, never let the vision and its core principles stray far from the mind of the school community. Refer to it whenever the opportunity presents itself and represent it around the school in the form of posters or images (see Cog 4.4 for a description of a possible poster).

A school vision may always appear to be just over the brow of the hill and never quite reachable, but don't lose patience or try to cut corners. It is the road towards achieving that vision that transforms a school.

Chapter 3

An Ethos of Care and Positive Relationships

Everyone who remembers his own education remembers teachers, not methods and techniques. The teacher is the kingpin of the educational situation.

Sidney Hook[1]

Sidney Hook places the importance of the teacher as a person above the impact of pedagogical practices and curriculum content. For me, the quality relationships that staff have with young people throughout every aspect of the school is *the* essential ingredient in the recipe for good learning and teaching.

How we care for the young people in our schools and the relationships we have with them, and the relationships they have with each other, are the most obvious ways that ethos is observed in a school setting. In Chapter 1 we looked at leadership and in Chapter 2 at vision. They are both major contributors towards a school ethos but can be subtle in terms of their effect on creating a positive school ethos. These two areas are chiefly focused on the systems and structures we put in place to ensure the school ethos is positive – for example, you may have visited a school, walked around and quickly formed a view about its ethos. Along the way, you may have picked up a few hints as to the type of leadership in the school, and I certainly hope you will have picked up on the vision. However, I am in no doubt that it is the relationships you will have noticed above all else and will have influenced your opinion.

This chapter differs from the first two in as much as it deals with the day-to-day and very visible behaviours of everyone in the school community. In many respects, the issues explored in Chapters 1 and 2 go some way to forming the relationships in schools. However, unlike leadership and vision, which are most

---

1   Sidney Hook, *Education for Modern Man: A New Perspective* (New York: Alfred A. Knopf, 1963), p. 231.

often driven primarily by school leaders, the quality of relationships must be driven and led by all staff, with contributions by students via mechanisms such as student voice.

In this chapter, we will delve into the development of an ethos of care and positive relationships:

- Cogs 3.1–3.3 set the scene for what we must know and understand before we can begin to explore ways to develop good relationships and a caring environment. These cogs will better equip you to answer the following questions:

  > What is the one thing I should consider if I want to remain calm in difficult situations with young people?

  > Is my school an unhappy or happy environment, and what tensions do I have to resolve if I am to create a happy school?

  > What factors influence adolescent behaviour, and why is it essential to know and understand them?

- Cogs 3.4–3.6 look at relationships in detail and introduce the 5M's of positive relationships. We will discuss the merits of vertical tutoring as a means to make and maintain positive relationships, explore the human brain and why an understanding of how it works can give us practical ways to manage positive working relationships, and consider restorative practices as a way to repair broken relationships. These cogs will enable you to answer the following questions:

  > How can we make and maintain good relationships in school? How can we make and maintain positive relationships around the school – as a teacher in the classroom and as a tutor (form tutor, home teacher, etc.)?

  > How do we manage relationships when they start to go wrong between student and student or student and member of staff?

  > How do we mend relationships that have broken down or move them on in a positive way, when appropriate?

- Cogs 3.7–3.9 focus on some of the tensions school leaders may face when managing relationships – for example, balancing the well-being and welfare of students against the well-being and welfare of staff. Within this context, we also explore sanctions and exclusions and consider possible models. These cogs will help you to answer the following questions:

> If we were to discuss relationships at departmental or senior team meetings, rather than behaviour, how might this change the tone and outcome of the discussion?

> Why might clear lines or boundaries for young people make them want to kick against them but at the same time make them feel safe?

> Why should we never resort to fixed-term exclusions?

● Cogs 3.10–3.12 address three areas – bullying, uniform and digital media – which are the source of problems in many schools and can easily sway our perceptions of a school ethos. We will also reflect on the extent to which these areas can add to tension and conflict which can be avoided or at least reduced. These cogs will better equip you to answer the following questions, which also serve as the title for each cog:

> What to do about bullying?

> Uniform – a necessity or a source of tension?

> How concerned should we be about digital and social media?

Cog 3.1: Learning doesn't come first

Throughout most of the nineties and certainly well into my academy years, the phrase that was bandied around the most was 'learning comes first'. No one questioned it. Surely, it was obvious that learning came first and schools were all about learning? Initially, I was cynical; there were too many buzzwords and phrases around and we didn't need yet another one.

Eventually, I succumbed to the pressure and got caught up in the empty rhetoric along with everyone else. However, during this time, I had a different mantra which has never left me. It has helped to kick-start my thinking over the years and has led me to the conclusion that 'relationships come first'. Before I tell you what my mantra is, I am going to take you back to my first years in teaching.

Early in my career, I accepted a job as a geography teacher in a school that would subsequently be branded by the *Mail on Sunday* as 'the worst school in Britain'. The school was always mentally and physically exhausting but those first few weeks were impossible. In theory, I was well equipped – I applied all of my four years' worth of BEd teaching techniques to motivate the students and win them over. Nothing worked. Until, that is, my head of department marched into class one day and whispered in my ear: 'Never argue with a child – you will never win.' His advice was more useful than any other behaviour management book I have ever read or any behaviour-related course I have ever attended. And I still use it today.

Now, I realise that this may strike you as an anticlimax – it is fairly simple, after all – but how many of us actually manage to apply it? For me, it is a precursor to the value statement mentioned in the previous chapter: we have to accept that our students are young people who are still not fully developed physically, mentally or emotionally. You cannot win a quarrel with someone who does not argue rationally – and, let's face it, that applies to most teenagers. So, don't waste your time disagreeing with them; take a step back and figure out another method to get your own way.

I can honestly say that things became infinitely easier when I absorbed what my head of department was telling me. I learned to take that step back and stay cool. When I congratulated a boy for having his head buried in an atlas, apparently working hard for most of the lesson, I remained composed when it turned out that he was cutting up a lump of cannabis the size of a cigarette packet and wrapping it into cling-filmed segments in time for break. I was calm when a girl, rather than staying for a detention, climbed out onto the third-floor window ledge (no more than six inches wide) and wouldn't come back in. It didn't always work out that way, though, and I felt close to losing control quite often. But invariably when I did, I began to realise that it was me who had escalated the situation. They were children and there was no reason to argue or get angry with them.

Arguing is just one of the many negative things we do that can get in the way of teaching and learning. It also affects our own well-being. Our responses and reactions to students' behaviours can affect us for hours, days, weeks and even months after the event, and therefore it is paramount that we respond in the most effective ways possible to de-escalate situations and maintain healthy relationships in the classroom.

Cog 3.2: Learning to juggle

Can you remember any sarcastic or cutting comment that a teacher made when you were at school? It might not sound like much now, but at the time – especially if you were at your most sensitive (in your early teens) – you may have been hurt to the core, possibly damaging you more than you realised at the time. Conversely, what were the qualities of the teachers you liked or respected? What did they do in the classroom to make you like and respect them? How did they behave outside the classroom?

The types of relationships we experience in school – from both teachers and other students – can have as much, if not more, impact on our lives as the subjects we study or the qualifications we obtain. Some of these experiences can be negative, whether it is a harsh comment made at a vulnerable time in our lives, an episode of bullying or a humiliating experience in a classroom. These incidents can chip away at our self-esteem, our confidence and our aspirations. It is vital, therefore, that we not only try to minimise the negative experiences that a child may have, but also to build their resilience and skills to cope with them effectively when they do happen. In short, there is a bit of juggling to be done.

I would love to work in a truly happy school: a school where students work and play together in a kind and non-threatening way, where staff and students get along with each other in a supportive and caring environment, where staff work well with each other as a team. If only that were the case. Would such a school encourage consistently meaningful learning experiences? Would mistakes or errors of judgement be ignored? How would it manage the frustrations, jealousies and annoyances that occur on a daily basis whenever groups of people live or work together?

Let us consider a more realistic and pragmatic set of statements than the ones outlined above:

- I would love to work in a mostly happy and productive school: a school where students may upset each other at times but mostly they are able to prevent issues from arising. And when conflicts do occur, they are able to resolve their differences before they become damaging.

- A school that doesn't have an extensive set of rules for students as these can shut down opportunities for them to make choices. Instead, it allows students to learn from their errors of judgement and use this experience to build good habits for life.

- A school where staff and students may have disagreements at times but they are few and far between. When disagreements do occur, the relationships that exist between students and staff are strong and trusting enough for them not to get in the way of learning and personal development; the relationships are based on mutual respect and take place in a supportive and caring environment.

- A school where all staff work effectively with each other as a professional and trusting team, accepting that we all have our quirks and foibles but having the emotional wherewithal to overcome annoyances and mistrust.

- A school where we accept that things can go wrong between people at times but where we are equipped with the habits, systems and processes to minimise any long-term detrimental effects and then get on with it.

So, how can we reduce the fluctuation between negative and positive experiences and maximise the well-being of all?

Ask any parent what they want for their child at school and one of the top three answers has got to be: 'I want my child to be happy.' This seems straightforward enough on the surface: a school should ensure that its students have happy experiences and send them home happy at the end of the day. But, of course, that is hardly the purpose – or, at least, not the sole purpose – of schooling. Schools exist to give children meaningful and life-changing learning experiences. They aim to do this in a positive way, which will encourage every young person to embrace each learning encounter and hopefully acquire knowledge, skills and good habits, which in turn will enable them to go out and flourish in their future lives.

How do we accomplish this? This is where the juggling becomes more intense. We might succeed, to some degree, if we use all our pedagogical skills and every ounce of personality we possess. We might be having a run of lessons that are going brilliantly until one child (intentionally or not) pulls a pin and a bad behaviour grenade goes off. The rest of the class desperately need that valuable information you have been providing and now someone is preventing that from happening. Frustration builds and potential conflict looms. Much of the time we are trying to engage young people in topics which, although we may cherish and recognise their importance, they may have no interest in. This leads to tensions in the classroom.

What is more, the tensions are not just confined to the classroom: we put rules in place across the school estate, partly to make all our lives easier and more congenial and partly for safety reasons. Young people don't always see it that way. We could give them free rein to run around the corridors to their heart's content, use abusive language when they are angry or allow them to sell sweets in bulk to other students at every opportunity, but we don't. Instead, there are rules in place to ensure that they do things they may not necessarily wish to do. Of course, this leads to more tension and more potential conflict. However, we rightly persevere with enforcing rules and teaching curriculum content because one of the things we are trying to accomplish is to prepare students for adult life and all the rules and expectations it will throw at them. Although we are always reminding our students of this, young people continue to resist. It is natural for them to want to find out things for themselves and not be constantly told what to do or not do. To borrow from Guy Claxton's terminology, we should be trying to develop all aspects of their 'learning muscles'.[2] Teaching them how to recognise and cope with boundaries is part of this.

There is another tension that head teachers have to consider – between managing exclusions (and other punitive measures) and ensuring the staff body feel supported. This is particularly significant in schools where things have gone spectacularly wrong. The three schools I have led have all had some of the highest fixed-term exclusion rates in the country when I started: over 400 exclusions a term with many being for more than 10 days. All of them had reactionary policies and practices. There was an expectation that all children should be able to behave in the same way and therefore the same rules applied to all. However, people are

2   Guy Claxton, *Building Learning Power: Helping People to Become Better Learners* (Bristol: TLO, 2002).

very different and have different needs. There will be some students who are not able to cope with certain rules or conditions, so we should take more time to consider the alternatives, especially as an average of 40 students per day are permanently excluded in England.[3]

When Rumney High School and Llanrumney High School amalgamated to become Eastern High, the fear was that the students from each school would fight each other. This didn't transpire, but when I arrived at the school a year later, it was the demoralised staff who were at each other's throats. So much attention had been focused on students who crossed the line that staff well-being and a positive whole-school ethos had been forgotten.

What I am attempting to illustrate here is that schools are veritable minefields of potential conflict, whether it is at the school gates, in the dining hall, in the classroom or out on the playing fields. The mines are never far below the surface, waiting to explode in a cacophony of raised voices, physical intimidation, sarcasm and long-term grudges. This can occur between students, between students and staff and between staff members; both students and members of staff can be responsible for instigating or escalating the incident.

Dealing with the disparity between what adults think is good for a young person and what the young person thinks is good for themselves is not always easy, yet it is manageable most of the time. It can be reduced to the point where incidents are kept to a minimum and, when they do arise, they are de-escalated and dealt with quickly. More importantly, we can develop measures and practices to ensure that these episodes are avoided or de-escalated without any lasting damage to the child.

So, how do we go about creating a mostly happy school? In the next cog, we will take a brief look at adolescence. We need to know who we are working with before we can look at changing our practice and creating a positive school ethos that will increase the well-being of staff and students.

---

3   Based on 7,894 exclusions in England in 2018/19. See: https://explore-education-statistics.service.gov.uk/find-statistics/permanent-and-fixed-period-exclusions-in-england.

Cog 3.3: Getting to grips with adolescents

Understanding the nature of adolescence is a central cog in developing a positive school ethos. There is so much we still don't know about brain development; however, as we have seen, it is essential we accept that young people are still growing. They will make errors of judgement, and it is our responsibility to work through them with our students and help them to learn from their mistakes. For this reason, I have always seen it as a priority to ensure that those of us working in schools acquire an understanding of how they mature and rediscover what we all went through while growing up. In doing so, we cultivate empathy and, hopefully, the competency and capacity to work more constructively with young people.

Since the nineties, a huge industry has built up around how we learn, much of it based on research and some sadly not. Many of us will have experienced (and may still be experiencing) some of the outcomes – for example, Thinking Skills, Brain Gym and preferred styles of learning (e.g. visual, auditory and kinaesthetic). Some of it has moved pedagogy on in the classroom and some has probably done more harm than good by confusing the picture.

What I am not going to deal with in any detail here is the science of brain development and how we learn. There is a lot to recommend – for example, Guy Claxton's 4R's of learning[4] and Carol Dweck's growth mindset,[5] but there is also much that just plain gets in the way – for example, learning styles. What I am going to address is how to create the right conditions for learning, which we need to have in place before we can even begin to think about developing a child's learning potential. This takes me back to how we began this chapter: it isn't learning that comes first, it is relationships and how we model positive ways to treat each other.

---

4   Claxton, *Building Learning Power.*
5   Carol S. Dweck, *Mindset: The New Psychology of Success* (New York: Ballantine Books, 2007).

A brief guide to neurodevelopment and adolescence

While all the investigations into how we learn were taking place, quietly in the background, outside of the school domain, there has been an explosion of research into infant neurodevelopment and the impact of adverse childhood experiences on future emotional and physical well-being, as well as the capacity to form healthy relationships with other people. These studies have the potential to take schools to another level in respect of meeting the needs of all young people.

We are often quick to dismiss a lot of the behaviours of teenagers as quirks of their age. When things get more serious, we seek to apportion blame to make sense of a difficult situation, ranging from external influences (such as poor parenting, the school ethos (believe it or not), friendship groups and society in general) to more internal possibilities (such as underlying psychosomatic issues, past traumas and believing the child to be intrinsically bad – he or she was born that way). The nurture versus nature argument is pretty much redundant these days as there is evidence that both have a strong impact on the physical, linguistic, conceptual and emotional changes that occur in a child between birth and adulthood.

I am going to explore three areas of childhood development research which highlight the potential challenges affecting our relationships with young people: adverse childhood experiences, the early onset of puberty and the role of dopamine.

Adverse childhood experiences

The cross-party report, *The 1001 Critical Days*, which outlines the importance of acting early to enhance outcomes for children, is an excellent place to start if you want to know more. It not only highlights the importance of the attachment patterns a newborn child can develop in their first 1,001 days but also the potential damage caused to connections in the brain during this crucial period. New synapses are being formed continuously in the brain: 'From birth to age 18 months, connections in the brain are created at a rate of a million per second! The earliest experiences shape a baby's brain development, and have a lifelong impact on that baby's mental and emotional health.'[6] While all these new synapses are being formed, others that are not needed or are not being used are being pruned away, thus creating a 'use it or lose it' scenario.

Babies are born with higher numbers of defensive synapses; our natural human instinct is to protect ourselves so we can survive with minimum pain. We all face bumps and potholes on the journey to becoming an adult. However, for some children there aren't just minor dips along the way; there are great chasms to traverse. For example, if a child in their early years becomes regularly hypervigilant due to neglect or household violence, the reasoning centre of their brain is not given the opportunity to develop. The neglected child won't have made the same attachments or bonds with their parents as other more cared for children, and this will affect how they bond with others – in some cases for the rest of their lives. The synapses related to bonding with others have been pared away.

While these connections can become hardwired, there is a growing body of research to suggest that there is a small window of opportunity in adolescence when there is a degree of neuroplasticity in the brain. This creates opportunities to effect positive outcomes in a teenager's neurodevelopment and promote their capacity to form positive relationships with others. This is no easy task; it very much depends on the degree of adverse experiences a child has had and the level of trauma associated with those experiences. We will look at some possible ways that schools can address this issue in the next three cogs.

2. The earlier onset of puberty

Adolescence is generally regarded as the period between the onset of puberty and adulthood. This definition is misleading, however, because puberty has been occurring increasingly earlier in most populations. As yet, the reasons are not entirely clear, although some indicators point towards the influence of diet and possibly obesity.[7] At the other end of adolescence, the settling down of our neurons and synapse connections and the accompanying emotional instability can

---

6   Andrea Leadsom, Frank Field, Paul Burstow and Caroline Lucas, *The 1001 Critical Days: The Importance of the Conception to Age Two Period. A Cross-Party Manifesto* (2013), p. 5. Available at: https://www.nwcscnsenate.nhs.uk/files/8614/7325/1138/1001cdmanifesto.pdf.
7   Chai Woodham, 'Why Kids Are Hitting Puberty Earlier Than Ever', *US News* (17 April 2015). Available at: https://health.usnews.com/health-news/health-wellness/articles/2015/04/17/why-kids-are-hitting-puberty-earlier-than-ever.

extend well into our twenties. For many young people, this means that adolescence doesn't end until they are 24.[8]

This has implications for schools. With the onset of puberty occurring earlier for some young people, certain children will appear physically older than they actually are mentally and emotionally. This can lead to us unconsciously treating these students as more psychologically mature than they in fact are. Our expectations for them are beyond what they are capable of achieving.

As adults, we are all guilty from time to time of placing adult expectations and behavioural sensibilities on to young people. In secondary schools, it is all too easy to demonise a young person – until reason sets in, we take a step back and remember that we are dealing with a 12-year-old child.

Unfortunately, this happens all the way down through primary schools and into nurseries, where multi-agency meetings are called by nursery managers to discuss the 'dangerous child' in their setting – the child in question being as young as 3 or 4. It is this type of demonisation that can lead to quick fire-fighting exclusions which do nothing for the child over the long term.

3. The intensity of dopamine flooding the adolescent brain

Shaking small electricity pylons and causing the wires to smack together to create blue flashes (ultimately blacking out half the town), dismantling fireworks to make bigger and better explosions (resulting in a hospital visit), go-karting down a steep hill with no brakes and crossing a major road, and climbing to the top of a castle ruin (even though several people had fallen and broken bones). These are just some of the many near-death stories from my own childhood.

Those were the days when children went outside to play and released all that risk-taking and thrill-seeking behaviour that goes hand in hand with adolescence. Of course, there are other types of risky adolescent behaviour such as substance misuse, criminal damage, physical assault, sexual exploration and, more recently, gaming. All of these carry with them various degrees of peril, danger and thrill. More worryingly, some of them can have lasting damage on the individual.

8   Susan M. Sawyer, Peter S. Azzopardi, Dakshitha Wickremarathne and George C. Patton, 'The Age of Adolescence', *Lancet Child Adolescent Health*, 2(3) (2018): 223–228. DOI:10.1016/S2352-4642(18)30022-1

Jane Anderson's article titled 'The Teenage Brain: Under Construction' explains how the adolescent brain is at a vulnerable stage in its development.[9] The prefrontal cortex (the reasoning part of the brain) is just starting to form and with this comes an increased surge in sex hormones (among others) and neurotransmitters like dopamine (which plays a role in how we feel pleasure). Dopamine levels change throughout adolescence, and research suggests that young people require more excitement and stimulation to achieve the same levels of pleasure as an adult.[10]

There is also evidence that greater levels of dopamine are released compared to adults when a young person partakes in addictive activities, such as drug and alcohol use, pornography, gaming and gambling.[11] In other words, there are higher rates of addiction to high-risk activities in young people than in adults. Young people can evaluate risk as well as adults; however, the intensity of dopamine flooding the brain can easily outweigh considerations of potential negative outcomes. Consequently, adolescence is a time of greatly increased impulsivity, sensation-seeking and risk-taking. The result of this appears to be the apparent inability to match behaviour to the likely rewards (or punishments) that might follow.

This makes it all the more difficult for schools, but hasn't it always been this way? Science is certainly helping us to understand the reasons for teenagers' behaviours and to make sense of a complex situation. For me, it highlights the need to place the emotional and psychological development of young people at the core of any school ethos. A failure to acknowledge this fact will prevent us from maximising the number of young people we can help to go on and flourish in life.

Introducing the 5M framework

The knowledge we now have of adolescence and adolescent development makes it easier to implement effective strategies which will create a positive ethos throughout the school and, in turn, enhance learning. In the following three cogs,

9 Jane Anderson, 'The Teenage Brain Under Construction', *American College of Paediatricians* (May 2016). Available at: https://acpeds.org/position-statements/the-teenage-brain-under-construction.
10 Adriana Galvan, 'Adolescent Development of the Reward System', *Frontiers in Human Neuroscience*, 4(6) (2010). Available at: https://www.ncbi.nlm.nih.gov/pmc/articles/PMC2826184.
11 Linda P. Spear, 'Adolescent Neurodevelopment', *Journal of Adolescent Health*, 52(2, Supp. 2) (2013): S7–13. DOI: 10.1016/j.jadohealth.2012.05.006

we will explore a framework we can use to develop a positive learning ethos within which young people can thrive. In essence, we adhere to five key principles (the 5M's) when we interact with our students, which are organised under three overarching categories.

The first category focuses on how we *make and maintain* good relationships as members of staff around the school, as teachers in classrooms and as tutors or pastoral staff (Cog. 3.4). It is all about the proactive things we do to foster positive relationships across every aspect of the school.

The second category deals with how we *manage* relationships if things begin to go wrong (Cog 3.5). We still have to accept that no matter how good relationships with our students are, things will go wrong at times. We can't mitigate for every experience a child may have and we certainly can't expect teaching staff to shake off at the classroom door every bit of discord we may have faced at home the night before or the worries we might have about our ever-growing overdraft. Sometimes we get it wrong, just as children do. That is when we need to draw on our capacity to manage difficult situations when relationships break down. This could be between a member of staff and a student or between student and student.

Finally, the third category focuses on how we *mend* relationships that have broken down, and if we don't think we can repair them fully, how we can *move* them on in a positive way (Cog 3.6).

Dive in and pick out anything you aren't yet addressing in your school.

Cog 3.4: Getting relationships right – making and maintaining

Good relationships enable us to encourage, motivate and engage young people, creating a favourable environment for effective learning to take place. Positive relationships also enable us to enjoy our work and the students to enjoy their time in school, resulting in increased levels of well-being for staff and students.

The first step to creating a congenial ethos is to focus on how we initiate positive relationships with young people and (if we get that right) how we foster and maintain those relationships on a day-to-day basis.

Young people are far more observant than we often give them credit for – they notice who cares. At times it may be conscious and sometimes unconscious, but they don't miss much. It never ceases to amaze me, when I am walking along a corridor, deep in thought, and a student will come up to me and ask why I am frowning. I should have learned by now, but I always forget, that although young people outwardly affect total nonchalance towards you, they do in fact want you to notice them and be there to look after them and care for their well-being.

Young people place a lot of trust in school staff. From the moment they first walk into the building, they are in a high state of vigilance. They are suddenly meeting lots of new people, forming relationships with these strangers and being judged by everyone they come across. All they have to protect them are the 'grown-ups' in the school.

Of course, as mentioned in Cog 3.3, their degree of vigilance will depend on their family environment and past school experiences, which will impact on how secure they feel. Young people draw on previous positive and negative experiences to help them manage new situations. For example, a student who doesn't get on with a particular teacher in Year 7 will take this with them into Year 8. They may form excellent relationships with their new teachers, bar the one teaching the subject they had a poor experience with in the previous year, even if it is a different individual. This teacher may find the child unforthcoming and unwilling to cooperate. They may also find that they are behind in their understanding of the subject. It takes a strong teacher to turn this around and form a constructive relationship.

It is easy for the teacher to take this personally and (unconsciously) begin to treat the child in a less congenial way than they might have done otherwise. As a result, the child may continue to dislike the subject and mistrust the teacher. If this happens with other student–teacher relationships in Year 7, then it is likely that the level of mistrust will grow year on year, leading to underachievement, poor behaviour and a young person with a very low self-image.

If we accept that young people are still developing, it is up to us to make and maintain positive relationships with the students in our care. It is by modelling good practice that we enable them to begin to develop these complex skills for themselves.

Let us look at three situations where we interact with students in school and explore some of the actions we should be taking to make and maintain positive relationships.

1. Making and maintaining everyday relationships around the school

Just as school leaders should model the behaviours they want to see in their staff, so all adults working in a school should model the behaviours and relationships they want to see in young people. This can take many forms but the following list should be non-negotiables:

- Acknowledging as many students as possible when we walk around the building.
- Knowing as many names as we can.
- Showing an interest.
- Reminding them of appropriate (non-confrontational) behaviour which shows you care.
- Accepting and/or admitting when you are wrong.

● A fresh start every time.

● Unconditional respect.

The first four points above focus on the importance of being noticed and noticing others. One of the first pieces of advice I give to early career teachers is how to manage the walk from the classroom to the staffroom: try to greet at least five students with a 'Hello' or 'Good morning'; aim to learn the names of any student you have an interaction with and address them from then on by name; try to comment on a game they are playing or any other activity in which they are involved; and always pick up on one or two misdemeanours you spot (e.g. a coat on in the corridor or a piece of dropped litter).

Following these suggestions is time and (potential) aggravation well invested, especially when persuading someone to pick up the rubbish they have just dropped. The teacher who eschews such behaviours will struggle to establish genuinely positive learning relationships, not only in the corridors but also in their own classroom. As we saw earlier, students know and recognise the members of staff who care. As long as there is consistency, the students will respect you as a teacher and/or school leader. Things then become a lot easier because your reputation precedes you.

The last three points above focus on the attributes you need to develop as a person to ensure that good relationships are maintained. It is about reliability, honesty, integrity and the ability to forgive and move on. If a student makes an error of judgement or does something wrong deliberately, we want them to admit it, accept responsibility and try to learn from their mistake. As adults, we must show them that we can do the same. As a head teacher, it is equally important to adopt this way of behaving with staff and students. Know when to back down and model the behaviours you want to see in others.

Students have short memories, so attempting to return to the point you were trying to make or settle a disagreement from the day before is pointless. There will be other ways and times to make your position clear. Instead, start each day afresh. If the student's behaviour deserved a sanction the day before, apply the appropriate punishment, but do it at the time and in a manner that is consistent with past sanctions you have applied. Require the same standards of behaviour you always expect to see, but do it from the perspective of a clean slate. If you come in still angry from the previous day and looking for trouble, events will quickly escalate – and from the point of view of the student, nothing will have been learned.

Another principle we need to adopt is to have unconditional respect for our students. Unconditional respect means there is no circumstance in which you will stop dealing with the student in a courteous manner. Young people need to know you respect them as a person. When they make a mistake or an error of judgement, they want to know that you will address the misdemeanour but in a fair way that shows you value them as an individual.

When maintaining good relationships, we should never say: 'I'm fed up with you' or 'You're really making me cross.' Instead, our comments should be behaviour and action focused: 'Running in the corridor is dangerous' or 'Running in the corridor is upsetting people.'

2. Making and maintaining everyday relationships as a teacher

Taking the time to consider how you can make and maintain good relationships with your students that are conducive to learning will set you well on your way to becoming an outstanding teacher.

If the relationships you have with your students in the classroom are constructive, you will be able to challenge and engage them far more easily and effectively than the teacher who doesn't invest in teacher–student relationships. Here are a few examples of the ways teaching staff can develop a good rapport with students:

- Assessing progress and giving feedback regularly.
- Knowing the specific needs of every student.
- Developing empathy for students.
- Active (empathic) listening.
- Developing an understanding of behavioural theories of attachment.[12]
- Providing relevant work to make it worth their while.
- Practise motivational strategies.

12 See, for example, Kendra Cherry, 'What Is Attachment Theory? The Importance of Early Emotional Bonds', *VeryWellMind* (17 July 2017). Available at: https://www.verywellmind.com/what-is-attachment-theory-2795337.

- Use of voice.

- Asking for regular feedback on your performance.

- Every day is a new day.

The first five points are about knowing your students well. Although I am not going to delve too deeply into assessment for learning, it is nevertheless something that every teacher needs to master. We assess student work and progress for three main reasons: to provide feedback which helps them know what to do to improve their work and/or progress further; to plan future learning sessions effectively (e.g. revisiting a topic the class hasn't quite understood); and, possibly the most important, to personalise or differentiate learning sessions effectively. There is a hidden benefit to all of this: the students will know that you care and are looking out for them.

While assessment provides teachers with one way of developing good working relationships with their students, it is nevertheless focused solely on the learning and how to enable them to progress. As with tutors (which we will explore in more detail on page 109), if they are to truly connect with their class then teachers also need to understand their students in a wider context. They need to be proactive in the ways they work with students, anticipating their needs and cutting off any potential lesson-disrupting mishaps.

This requires a certain degree of empathy. I realise there is only so much a teacher can do; however, if we are looking to develop our staff, then two useful tools to provide them with are a good understanding of behavioural theories (such as attachment theory or adolescent developmental theories) and skills which will develop greater levels of empathy and understanding (such as empathetic listening techniques).

The first will foster a degree of empathy and help them to understand why certain students are acting in certain ways. This will not only enable the teacher to respond appropriately, but as they come to understand the context of each student it will also help them to de-stress. The second goes even further in helping teaching staff to get to know their students. Taking the time to listen empathetically to individuals who may be causing a problem in the class has three benefits: the students respect the fact that they are being listened to, the teacher gains a better understanding of the students' needs, and things may be revealed that will help the teacher or someone else to meet those needs.

We should always aim to listen with empathy to what our students are saying – their comments, responses, complaints and witty remarks. There are often hidden warnings to back off or just let me be in this lesson. The more we are aware of these signals, the better we can maintain good working relationships.

There will be opportunities to speak to the student after the lesson or perhaps after school in a detention, but a word of warning: don't try to take on the role of a counsellor if you haven't been properly trained. I have fallen into the trap a few times in my career of believing that I can help a child by being the person who will listen to him or her. It can end up with the child becoming over-reliant on you, and because you haven't set the necessary rules and boundaries (such as times to meet), you can end up letting the child down. It is more important to recognise when to refer on.

The final five points above are more related to teaching and learning. As a rule, we don't do enough to make the work we do as relevant to our students' lives as possible, both in terms of content and skill/disposition development. A project-based curriculum dealing with authentic issues really does motivate young people.

The importance of voice is obvious: we need to sound genuine and behave consistently. A teacher who suddenly shouts aggressively and then the next minute is talking quietly leaves young people confused and kick-starts the defence mechanisms of those already on a high state of alert. Keep it calm and quiet. Yes, you can raise your voice to be heard but never in a hostile way. And never use words or phrases that directly attack the child, such as 'Shut up!' Do I need to mention sarcasm? It never works.

Finally, ask the students what they think of you. A student feedback card, which teachers can hand out to all their students to fill in before they leave the lesson, is a simple way to canvass their views.

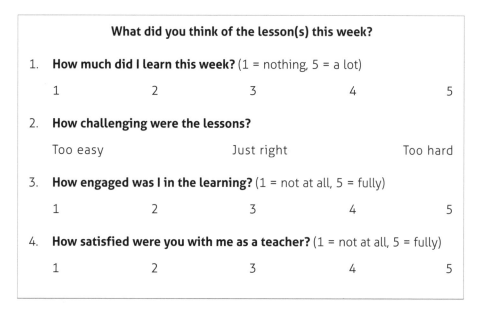

We haven't forced teachers to use feedback cards and the responses are totally confidential. However, they not only help the teacher to become more aware of their own performance, but they also help to foster good relationships. Young people appreciate being asked for their opinion.

3. Making and maintaining everyday relationships as a tutor

Much of what I have said above concerning staff behaviours around the school and in the classroom are applicable to the role of the form tutor, but it is worth mentioning a few points that are specific to the tutor. My definition of a form tutor, for the purposes of this book, is the person with responsibility for meeting with cohorts of students for short periods once or twice a day, carrying out duties such as registration, attending to welfare/well-being needs and developing personal and social education. Tutor groups are traditionally organised into same-age groupings (horizontal tutoring), although many schools now populate their tutor groups with students from multiple year groups (vertical tutoring – we will look at this in more detail below). In British secondary schools, the form tutor is normally the first point of contact with the parents of their group of students.

The form tutor normally has a closer relationship with their tutees than subject teachers. The tutor focuses more holistically on the needs of the child and makes and maintains relationships by:

- Carrying out regular group discussion sessions – for example, circle time.[13]

- Actively observing, supporting and referring where appropriate.

- Being accessible and responsive to students' needs (the tutee should always know where the tutor is).

- Having an active interest in the students' progress.

- Keeping in close contact with home – the home–school link.

This list of activities can take on a new meaning when carried out within a vertical tutoring (VT) framework. Before describing VT, I would like to mention Peter Barnard who introduced me to it. Following a career as a successful head teacher, Peter has since dedicated his time to developing the role of school leaders and the tutor within a multi-age, VT context, and at the time of writing he continues to do so. He has written five books on the subject which are far better than anything I can say on the matter, so if VT interests you, I would certainly consider investigating his work further.[14]

By establishing efficient practices and systems which enable effective learning, Peter's systems have enabled me to shift the ethos in three secondary schools in my role as head teacher. Under this model, the tutor becomes central to the whole system and every member of staff in the school can become a form tutor. In this way, it becomes easier to monitor and support students.

We have two tutors in every tutor group – normally one teacher paired with a non-teaching member of staff – and we try to keep the groups to fewer than 20 students. This allows one tutor to mentor and/or carry out year-based activities (don't forget there will be around four to six students from each year group in each tutor group), while the other tutor leads any tutor-based activities. Our assemblies are also vertical, as we have found this to be far more effective, although there is

---

13 For a good introduction to circle time see: Jenny Mosley, *Quality Circle Time in the Secondary School: A Handbook of Good Practice*, 2nd edn (Abingdon and New York: Routledge, 2013).
14 See www.verticaltutoring.org.

occasionally the need for a year-based assembly. At Eastern High, the tutor groups (we call them 'learning families') meet twice a day, once during the day for normal tutor-based activities and once at the end of the day for homework activities, with one-to-one pastoral support taking place.

This set-up allows us to make and maintain close relationships throughout the school: the tutor plays a central role in monitoring and supporting a small group of students, while the students have a greater sense of security and belonging. It also allows us to develop good relationships with parents, as the tutor becomes the primary source of information regarding their tutees. Furthermore, the tutor can focus on a few students in a year group at key times of the year – for example, transition into Year 7, Year 8/9 options and Year 11 exam preparation. We carry out a staggered system of year-based progress reports (three times per year) which provides an opportunity to offer more intensive review/evaluation sessions with the students.

In accordance with Peter's advice, we never give the tutors activities to carry out that will affect their relationship with the tutees. There is no need to put them through the torture of spaghetti tower-building type exercises or dull 'this is how you ought to behave' activities, which can so easily lead to situations where the tutor ends up in conflict with some of the group.

Instead, it is all about monitoring, support and guidance. For example, our student induction at the start of the academic year is very quick. Following welcome assemblies, the Year 11s meet and greet the Year 7s from their learning family and take them to their learning family room, where they are introduced to the rest of the tutor group, take part in a circle time session and encounter the usual organi-sational activities, such as giving out timetables, ensuring everyone knows where they are going and what equipment they need on what days. They are then straight on to the first lesson of the day.

Circle time is a powerful tool for tutors. Regularly taking the time to sit the class in a circle and explore how they are feeling about school and their relationships with each other is a fantastic way to make and maintain good relationships, not only between the tutor and the students but also between the students. It is time well invested.

Cog 3.5: Getting relationships right – managing relationships when they start to go wrong

We can do everything in our capacity to ensure we make and maintain good relationships, but:

- We are all human and we all make mistakes and errors of judgement.

- We are working with young people who also make mistakes and errors of judgement (just a little more often).

- We can't be accountable for all the millions of interactions that take place in schools on a daily basis.

Things will sometimes go wrong. So, how do we minimise any adverse impact when negative incidents occur? For me (and the schools in which I have worked), the answer came when I was first introduced to 'red zones' and 'blue zones'.

John Corrigan is the founder and a director of Group 8 Education, an Australian company who came to work with us at Bristol Brunel Academy. At the time, they had an excellent coaching programme for senior leaders, focusing on how we cope with stress and our associated behaviours. John introduced us to the concept of red and blue zones in the brain, each of which sparks associated behaviours, which we will look at below.

Corrigan explains the concept of red and blue states of mind in more detail in *The Success Zone*[15] and in *Red Brain Blue Brain*,[16] which describes the order in which he

---

15 Andrew Mowat, John Corrigan and Doug Long, *The Success Zone: 5 Powerful Steps to Growing Yourself and Leading Others* (Mount Evelyn, VIC: Global Publishing, 2009). If you are interested in finding out how to apply red and blue zones in your school, this book is an excellent place to start.
16 John Corrigan, *Red Brain Blue Brain: Living, Loving and Leading without Fear* (Leichhardt, NSW: Castleflag, 2019). This book focuses particularly on the practices that can be used to regulate, manage and ultimately entirely remove the red brain (i.e. the red zone).

believes our layered brain develops. His model is essentially a simplification of the functions of the limbic system and prefrontal cortex.

The limbic system, situated deep inside the brain, is responsible for our behavioural and emotional responses. The amygdala is particularly relevant here as it 'helps coordinate responses to things in your environment, especially those that trigger an emotional response. The structure plays an important role in fear and anger.'[17] If we jump when we hear a loud or unexpected noise, this is the amygdala responding. The prefrontal cortex is essentially the rational, thinking part of the brain. In children, the prefrontal cortex isn't fully developed, hence the reason why a child or teenager will slip into a rage far more quickly than most adults. Sometimes these parts will work together and sometimes they will work in isolation; for instance, a child presenting with challenging behaviours will likely be drawing mostly on the limbic system.

Corrigan believes that most humans experience their lives through these two brain states. For example:

Red brain states	Blue brain states
Negative feelings emerge.	Regulate impulses.
Our focus narrows.	Confident.
Ruminate over past events.	Collaborative.
Indulge in negative self-talk.	Empathic.
Uncontrolled rage at most extreme.	Creative.
Complete apathy and withdrawal.	Self-directed.
We have limited control over ourselves.	Self-motivated.

17 Jill Seladi-Schulman, 'What Part of the Brain Controls Emotions?', *Healthline* (23 July 2018). Available at: www.healthline.com/health/what-part-of-the-brain-controls-emotions.

Let us consider the following two scenarios:

1. When conflict arises between two (or more) students

Fights between students in schools do happen. Regardless of the school, having a thousand adolescents interacting in a thousand different ways will sometimes result in varying degrees of discord. I always mention this to parents during Year 6 open evenings and was once reprimanded by a chair of governors who told me that I shouldn't allude to this because 'We don't want parents thinking we have fighting in our school!' My reason for being open to parents is because I believe that they appreciate the honesty. What parents really want to know is how well prepared we are to deal with any potential fight before it escalates.

I have dealt with countless conflicts over the years. What I find most interesting about them is that, more often than not, if staff keep out of the way then an actual physical fight doesn't occur. Now, I am not saying this is always the case. However, there have been numerous occasions when I have been walking around the school and spot the beginnings of a disagreement. As usual, a few people begin to gather and the argument intensifies. If I go across and intervene then a physical fight will likely break out, but if I stay out of the way it will probably die down. I have experimented with this hypothesis many times, and every time that I (or another member of staff) intervene, one or both of the potential combatants loses their temper – always dramatically – and goes for the other student.

I have asked various students about my theory. Many of them admit that the reason they are happy to argue to the point of a fight breaking out (when in school) is that they know it will be broken up by a member of staff, and so neither party loses face. Out in the community, quite a few (mainly boys) have said that they don't get into arguments and, in fact, actively avoid fighting because they don't know if the other person is carrying a weapon. This a PhD topic in the waiting for someone! We need to bear this in mind when managing a potential or actual conflict: young people don't want to fight but they also don't want to be humiliated.

The key word when managing conflict is *calm*.

- **Be aware of the zone you are in.** You need to keep those fingers over your thumb (I will explain this shortly) and remain in the blue zone and in control of your own emotions.

- **Never run to a fight or argument to break it up.** As we discussed in Cog 1.3, not only will this increase the tension, but it will also signal to every student in the area that something exciting is about to happen, and before you know it, you have 50 students following you. If three other teachers approach from different directions, that is 150 students gathered round.

- **Keep your voice calm and quiet.** Shouting only heightens the tension and will excite the students around you.

- **Defuse the situation.** Help the students to make sense of what is going on by gently reflecting back to them the feelings underlying their thoughts, words and behaviour. Admittedly, this can be challenging when in a state of high stress.

- **Disperse the audience.** Again, this should be done quietly and without threats. If there are too many students around, guide the angriest combatant (who by this time will normally be stomping off somewhere with the crowd ready to follow) into a room to separate them.

- **Positive handling.** Sometimes you may have to resort to safe holding techniques, but you should only do so when a child is in danger of being hurt. I have been approached many times by staff asking for whole-staff positive handling training and I have always politely refused. My reason for this is that trained staff are more likely to be overconfident and possibly even look for opportunities to use their new-found skills. Our approach is to train key staff members only (e.g. SLT and possibly house leaders). We advise other staff to use their judgement and only intervene when there is the possibility of a student harming either themself or others, and only if they feel sufficiently confident that they can do this in a calm and measured manner that will cause no injury to the young person.

- **Restorative conversations.** These usually happen after the event and are the subject of the fourth M (moving on in a positive way), However, occasionally a quick restorative conversation will defuse things straight away, if the timing is right and the adversaries haven't tipped into the red zone: 'Okay, one at a time ... What's happened? ... What were you thinking when this happened? ... What can we do to put things right?'

2. Between students and members of staff

Most incidents where a student has been removed from the classroom by a duty member of staff could have been avoided. This may sound unreasonable to some staff, but when a duty call is made, it is most often the teacher who has prompted the escalation. And, usually, the teacher is in the red zone.

In an attempt to de-escalate tensions, I have one golden rule that I always repeat to my students: 'Never, ever argue with a teacher.' I might go on to elaborate: 'If the teacher is asking you to move seats because they think you are talking, there are two possibilities: first, the teacher is correct and you are guilty. In this case, be big about it. You have been caught. Just apologise and move. For 99.9% of the time the teacher will let it go at that. Keep pleading your innocence and refusing to move and it will escalate. Second, the teacher is genuinely in the wrong and you weren't talking. In this case, just move, but in a calm voice say to the teacher: "Miss, I'll move, but I wasn't talking. Can I talk to you about it at the end of the lesson?" This is how to be calmly assertive and grown up. For 99.9% of the time that will be the end of the matter. And, as an added bonus, you haven't lost face in front of the rest of the class. In fact they will respect you for it.'

Similarly, as we saw in Cog 3.1, I give the same message to my teachers: 'Never argue with a child – you will never win.' Instead, let them know the behaviour is unacceptable and that you will deal with it, either when you have attended to the rest of the class or by calling for support and possible removal from the room.

A steady drip-feed of reminders in student assemblies and staff briefings goes some way to ensuring that these rules are adhered to, but we all know that it doesn't always work. For example, a young person can fly into the red zone very quickly, a member of staff can make the initial accusation in a red way rather than a calm and measured blue way, there is a full moon, it is rainy/windy or there is a wasp in the room.

Staying predominantly in the blue zone is not easy, especially for young people. One way to raise self-awareness is to work towards a Blue Zone Day for the school. In the lead-up to it, survey staff and students at the end of each day, asking them how often they were in the red zone and what they did to move back into the blue zone. This can be done electronically for staff and (if they have the devices) students, or alternatively, in a homework planner or other paper journal. Every day, the tactics that staff and students use to move into the blue zone can be shared anonymously. On Blue Zone Day itself, the hope is that both staff and students have developed enough awareness during the preceding weeks to be in the blue zone for the whole day.

One trick we share with staff when they feel they are losing control is to imagine their thumb is the reptilian brain (red zone); their arm could be seen as the spinal cord in this context. They should place their thumb so that it lies in the palm of the same hand and cover it with their fingers, which represents the emotional and thinking brain (blue zone), as in the illustration below.

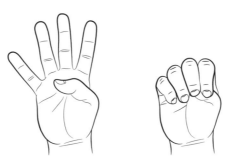

When your fingers are not covering your thumb you have 'flipped your lid', so the idea is to close the lid on your red reptilian brain and move back into the blue zone. It is a simple tool to help you focus on your state of mind, but I find myself using it hundreds of times a day – it really does help. Many staff also use this technique to good effect.

The key points to remember when relationships begin to break down between staff and students are as follows:

- **Accept that the student is young and will make mistakes.** Don't forget that you are working with children. Familiarise yourself with child development theories and keep in mind all of the factors that relate to adolescence. Developing empathy will keep you on the right side of the red/blue zone divide.

- **Stay in the blue zone.** There are times when a bit of the red zone comes into play – your human side. Sometimes it is helpful to let young people see that part so they know they have upset you. However, you need to be conscious of which zone you are in and pull yourself back into the blue if you want to maintain control in front of the students.

- **Consistency in approach.** If you are inconsistent in the way you approach behaviour issues, you will quickly lose the respect of the students. Again, an awareness of which zone you are in is vital. You may have woken up late, your own child may be ill at home and half their breakfast is down your shirt, but this shouldn't colour the way you deal with an uncooperative child in school. It is not their fault that you are having a bad day. Don't forget that they will spot any change in approach instantly and they will certainly notice your mood.

- **Develop an ethos of reflective practice.** Give the student time and space to reflect on their behaviour before intervening. Quietly point out the misdemeanour in such a way that they are not in danger of losing face in front of their peers. You need to allow them the chance to back down of their own accord. Likewise, sometimes you will need the option of backing off and reflecting yourself. Maybe you have got it wrong and inadvertently made a false accusation. If this is the case, admit you were wrong and apologise. It is always appreciated by young people and will make them more cooperative in the future as they know they can trust you.

- **Clarity and consistency with regards to consequences.** None of what I have said so far necessitates us doing away with sanctions. Young people still need boundaries and to face the consequences for unacceptable behaviour. However, we need to ensure that they learn from their mistakes, so any repercussions should be meaningful and related to the misbehaviour – for example, restorative meetings, restricted or no access to an item that has been damaged, detentions or workshops (related to the misdemeanour) rather than fixed-term exclusions, and unconditional positive regard shown throughout any reprimand. Whatever the sanction, make sure the students know why they are receiving it and that its application is consistent with your school behaviour policy.

- **Avoid any identified personalised responses (where appropriate).** Focus on the behaviour, not the person. Sarcasm or reminders that certain individuals are always misbehaving are inappropriate as it focuses on the child rather than their actions.

Cog 3.6: Getting relationships right – mending and/or moving on

Of all the varied approaches that contribute to a positive school environment in which relationships are nurtured and maintained, restorative practices are the glue that holds them together. We usually turn to restorative practices to repair damaged relationships – that is, we encourage students to take responsibility for their behaviour by thinking about the causes and consequences – although restorative approaches can also be used as a preventative measure. However, it is not, and nor should it be, a catch-all for all aspects of making, maintaining and managing relationships.

Restorative practices: a reactive model with proactive outcomes

Restorative approaches/restorative solutions/restorative justice (it has had many labels) began as a project to bring together victims and perpetrators of crime as far back as the 1970s (although the term was first coined in the first half of the 19th century). In the UK, it really took off in the nineties when the criminal justice system began using face-to-face mediation to repair the harm caused to victims of crime – that is, a reactive process which takes place after the event.

The word restorative comes from restore – 'to put things right'. So, restorative approaches are practices you use to rebuild relationships that have broken down – ideally to the point that they can be fully repaired or at least to the point where all the parties concerned can get on with their lives in the same community without fear for their safety or the threat of reprisals.

Defining restorative approaches

The Crown Prosecution Service defines restorative justice as follows:

- Victim satisfaction: To reduce the fear of the victim and ensure they feel 'paid back' for the harm that has been done to them.

- Engagement with the perpetrator: To ensure that they are aware of the consequences of their actions, have the opportunity to make reparation, and agree a plan for their restoration in the community.

- Creation of community capital: To increase public confidence in the criminal justice system and other agencies with a responsibility for delivering a response to antisocial behaviour.[18]

In schools we might interpret this as:

- Victim satisfaction: reducing victim fear by listening and taking appropriate action (against the perpetrator if necessary) to ensure the victim feels secure and satisfied that there will be no repetition of the behaviours that led to this.

- Engagement with the perpetrator: to ensure they understand the consequences of their actions and have the opportunity to make reparation. Or, if both students feel aggrieved (as is most often the case in schools), then there is an opportunity for them both to accept mutual responsibility and agree a plan to move forward.

- Creation of community capital: to increase school and wider community confidence in how incidents are dealt with effectively by the school.

By all means adopt restorative approaches but keep it simple and in line with the principles and values underlying your school. It is about restoring and mending relationships so that those involved can resume their previous relationship or

18 Crown Prosecution Service, 'Restorative Justice' (24 September 2019). Available at: https://www.cps.gov.uk/legal-guidance/restorative-justice.

agree to go their separate ways, but done in an amicable way without any fear of retaliation from either side. At Eastern High, it is part of our sustainability framework (sustainable relationships and partnerships). We have adopted many practices, with restorative approaches being just one part of this framework. It is not the guiding force behind the school, although it is a very useful tool.

Using restorative approaches in schools

Restorative approaches can be used in various ways to help mend or move on relationships that have broken down. In this section we will consider informal discussions/conversations and formal meetings.

Restorative discussions/conversations (informal)

Restorative discussions occur most often when an immediate situation is brewing. Many schools issue their staff with cards containing a script to follow. It will contain a number of questions aimed at both parties. The scripts vary slightly depending on the school but they all run along the lines of:

- What happened?
- What were you thinking/feeling at the time?
- How do you feel now?/What has been hardest for you?
- How have others been affected?
- What do you think you need in order to make things right?

These scripts can be very useful and help to develop consistency across the school, but they come with a warning: staff will need to know more about the techniques and principles underlying the approach for restorative practices to be effective. For example, the principle of restorative conversations is not to replace sanctions entirely, but they can certainly reduce them if done well. In the case of techniques, one useful skill to develop with staff is active or empathic/active listening.[19]

---

19 For a good introduction to empathic listening see: Richard Salem, 'Empathic Listening', *Beyond Intractability* (July 2003). Available at: https://www.beyondintractability.org/essay/empathic_listening.

In schools where restorative approaches have been introduced, there comes a point when the students start coming to the staff to ask for a restorative meeting. That is when you know it is becoming well established. However, when it is initially introduced, you will hear a lot of impatient sighing from the students, mainly because teaching staff feel uncomfortable about the scripts initially and tend to read them in a rather mechanical way. Staff need time and practice for the scripts to become natural and spontaneous. When this happens consistently, the scripts become part of the fabric of the school and the students (although they would never admit it openly) come to appreciate the value of restorative conversations. It might take three years to get to this point, but it is time well spent.

Restorative meetings or conferences (formal) – between students or individuals and/or groups

Formal restorative meetings (involving two to four people) or conferences (with larger groups) are usually held by impartial staff who have more experience and training. You do not need to train all of your staff to this level. These meetings are particularly effective when you are trying to unravel a complex or long-running situation. Occasionally, these ongoing feuds require quite a few meetings over time and staff may begin to give up. Be resilient – they usually work in the end.

Don't forget that the meeting is about mending or moving on relationships. It is important for the parties involved to accept that there isn't necessarily going to be love and harmony following a conversation. Sometimes it is enough that there will be no resumption of hostilities and they may agree to go their separate ways. Often, one of the parties will need additional support afterwards to feel comfortable and begin afresh with new friends.

Restorative meetings or conferences (formal) – between student(s) and a member of staff

One of the aspects of restorative meetings that I haven't mentioned yet is that each party has to agree to be involved without coercion. Most students don't want to do it initially, but when they realise that it is a way of avoiding sanctions they tend to agree. Eventually, they see the value in the process and dodging a sanction is no longer the main motive for taking part in the conversation.

It is similar with staff when you are asking them to sit with a young person who has been systematically sending them into the red zone for the past four weeks. They often recoil at the thought and convey a whole host of emotions, ranging from affront ('Am I in trouble?' 'It's not my fault!') to genuine apologetic tears ('Am I to blame?').

It is vital, therefore, that these meetings are overseen by your best trained and/or most experienced members of staff. They do not need to be a member of the SLT – in fact, it is often better if they are not. Senior staff involvement can bring a coercive air to the proceedings, where things are said more to please the SLT member than to help repair the relationship. The member of staff also needs to be trusted and discreet. As with students, if restorative meetings are done well, staff will soon start to ask for them.

Other formal meetings

Restorative meetings or conferences can also be held between groups of parents or between staff. In the case of parents, these must be led by your very best trained members of staff – most often, a senior leader. These meetings tend to occur when there is an issue between families that is spilling over into the life of the school. They can be delicate and may often need external services to be represented, such as a family liaison officer or social worker. Nevertheless, they can have a tremendously positive impact, not only for the families concerned but for the school and community too. They can also develop a deeper level of trust between the school and its catchment area.

Restorative meetings between staff often come about at the request of a member of staff. They don't happen often but when they do they can help to recover what could have developed into a toxic staffroom atmosphere. Sometimes a nudge is required in the form of a reminder that restorative meetings are available for staff as well as students.

Many of you will have come across some of the practices described in Cogs 3.4– 3.6, which I have ascribed to the 5M framework. While these practices have served me well, what is more important is the overarching framework they sit within. Keeping the 5M's to the forefront of your mind when interacting with young people will help you to draw on the appropriate tools, skills and knowledge (some of which I have covered here and some of which you will discover for yourself) to enable positive and constructive relationships between staff, between staff and students, and between students and other students.

However, the question remains: how do we make these practices habitual for ourselves and the institution as a whole? How do we embed the 5M framework in order to create a culture and ethos that is conducive to learning on a day-to-day basis? The simple answer is time, endless repetition and constant modelling – day in, day out. If there isn't a dogged insistence on seeing something through, it will invariably fizzle out, so make sure you have some completer finishers in your senior team and back them up with a group of staff champions who will keep pushing the 5M's and their underpinning practices.

Furthermore, don't make the mistake of giving up on the 5M framework just because it doesn't always go according to plan. It won't. You will need to have in place a clear system of sanctions to support all the amazing relationships you are developing. There will always be instances that require more than a restorative conversation and where sanctions must be applied. We will explore this in the next cog.

Cog 3.7: The insecurities of behaviour management

There is always pressure from senior leaders to ensure that behaviour in school is well disciplined. When things go wrong, even if preventative and restorative measures are in place, a minority of the SLT may be demanding that strong action is taken against a student. One incident can lead to talk among teaching staff and soon everyone is having difficulty with them.

Occasionally, what starts as talk about one child can soon escalate to include an entire class, year group or, at an extreme, the whole school. If grievances of this type are shared among staff, it doesn't take long before another incident (e.g. a fight breaking out between two students) leads to comments such as, 'Behaviour is getting worse – it's not what it used to be,' 'Staff morale is low at the moment,' 'Something needs to be done about the behaviour in this school' and 'That child needs to be excluded.'

My personal insecurities feed happily on comments like these. I used to feel it as a deputy, but as a head it as if someone is stabbing you in the stomach. It is all too easy for head teachers to panic and introduce some draconian new rules or a sanction-heavy system of zero tolerance. I learned a lot from seeing this happen in schools where I worked early on in my career.

As a relatively new teacher at Hammersmith School, a challenging school in West London, I used to be one of those people in the staffroom berating senior leadership because behaviour in the school was so bad. We all did. Blaming others was painless and we validated our opinions through strength in numbers. It would have been alien for me at that time to think that we had a collective responsibility.

In a way, the senior team compounded the problem by over-reacting to staff criticisms. We seemed to have a new behaviour policy or system every half-term. Many different organisations and consultants were brought in, each one superseding the organisation or consultant who had let us down before. They all claimed to have the panacea for our problems. And all of them, over time, failed our school – and many others too, I imagine. Each botched behaviour initiative confirmed for us that we had lots of 'unteachable' students (which was not true) in the school and the support mechanisms in place (i.e. the senior team) were not up to the job.

Part of the problem was that these organisations and consultants had some excellent tools, tips and techniques, but they tended to be tools, tips and tricks that didn't explore the 'why' or link it to the ethos and principles supporting the school vision. For example, it seems sensible that rules should be written in positive language, but why? What is the thinking behind it? How could we use this to make the rules work more effectively?

Had we explored the idea of affirmative language more fully, perhaps we would have begun to genuinely develop the individual values of our school. This, in turn, might have led us to explore how positive behaviours could be introduced into other aspects of school life, which otherwise were in conflict with the positive language embedded in our rules. For example, take a rule such as: 'Walk quietly in corridors.' If a student is running noisily down a corridor, what contradictory messages are given to the student when a member of staff starts shouting at the top of his or her voice for them to stop. Worse still, what if the member of staff starts running after the student, perhaps thinking a fight is about to start? It is a simple example, but there has to be consistency of ethos across the whole school. But this takes time. It is not enough to introduce a new methodology and assume it will fit neatly into the values the school currently holds.

At this school, we didn't want to hear that practices take time (sometimes years) to become embedded and part of the day-to-day culture. Instead, we demanded a mass of tricks and practices to pull out of our hats at the appropriate time. However, they were all unrelated and didn't help when it came to entrenching consistent practice. When we did try systems that involved clear steps before we called for SLT support (that is, when codes are given to certain behaviours which build up sanction by sanction until a duty member of staff is called), incidents would escalate to such a degree that it would look as if behaviour was worse than ever, and so little by little the initiative would fade away. This engenders a sense of helplessness in teachers.

Giving staff a set of preordained rules and ways to apply them is never going to work, at least not in the long term. We need to develop these ourselves. It is no wonder that schools still pay out thousands of pounds for off-the-shelf behaviour management solutions, but still have staff in the staffroom complaining about behaviour on a daily basis and still fixed-term exclude frequently. It is also no surprise that staff turn senior leadership into scapegoats when it all goes wrong, especially when sets of rules within schools are created within reactive systems and are led from above with little staff and/or student consultation.

It is not easy to get behaviour policies right in schools in challenging circum-stances, where new issues arise on a daily basis, many which come into the school from the community and leave staff feeling vulnerable and insecure. Naturally, they will question the behaviour system, and we are again back to balancing staff sensitivities against student needs.

We will consider possible behaviour systems in the next cog, but before doing so I have two pieces of advice: firstly, make staff aware of the types of event that may happen. Prediction can be a powerful tool and will reassure staff that such inci-dents are not out of the ordinary. Secondly, ensure staff understand why events happen. Being able to provide an explanation helps staff to make sense of situa-tions and, again, appreciate that they are not extraordinary; they happen in all schools to some extent, more so in some and less so in others.

For the remainder of this cog, we will explore some examples of the types of behaviour-related incidents that can happen in schools.

The anatomy of a school year

In every school where I have worked, the following cycle has played out over the course of the year. I am sure you will recognise it. Nevertheless, when things get tough, staff (including the leadership team) often forget that the difficulties they face are not exclusive to their school. Instead, they may be quick to place the blame on some aspect of the school, such as its structures or leadership. This can lead to discontent and low staff morale. It is important, therefore, that you and your staff are aware of this cycle and reminded of it often. It is encouraging to know that you are not the only school finding it hard.

- **Renewing relationships.** The staff arrive back after the summer break full of energy and with big hopes and plans for the coming year. The students also return and, having been away from you and each other for so long, they take time to settle back in, regain their trust in you and rediscover the boundaries they have learned (this can take the entire month of September). This also applies to relationships with their peers. Everyone thinks the Year 7s are perfect and let them off with blue murder. (Why, oh why do we allow ourselves to be lulled into a false sense of security each year!)

- **Testing the boundaries and levels of trust.** After three or four weeks, you are paid a huge compliment: the students trust you again. However, this also means that they start to properly test the boundaries. This process also occurs with their peers, especially the Year 7s who have yet to establish a pecking order in their year group (this usually starts a bit later in mid-October or November).

- **Fatigue and wet weather.** Everyone begins to get tired two weeks before half-term when all the carefully planned lessons which were organised when the staff were full of energy are beginning to run out. The October break arrives and offers a slight reprieve, but with November, the dark nights set in and the mood begins to deteriorate. With this comes more angst-ridden lessons where the students are just not helping. At the same time, Year 8 have established their dominance over Year 7, who at the same time have been establishing their own hierarchy via fights and squabbles. All this leads to exaggerated talk among staff about how Year 8 are heading towards being the worst year group ever.

- **Christmas beckons.** The general mood in the school reaches a low at the start of December. However, from around the second week in December the holidays are in sight: people start giving each other cards, there are school performances and the Christmas tree goes up. It is a nightmare trying to stop staff from playing videos before the last couple of days, but apart from that things feel settled.

- **Deep dark winter and the January blues.** There may be problems when the students return, especially in schools where there are large numbers of child protection cases or in areas of high deprivation where students find themselves unable to cope having had particularly bad experiences over Christmas. (This may occur before the break, too, as students anticipate what might happen.) There may also be community-based incidents that spill over into school when everyone arrives back. The mood and behaviour doesn't take long to deteriorate in January. Everyone has a touch of sunlight deprivation and January never wants to end. On top of that, everyone is stuck inside on most days due to poor weather. Things are at their hardest from the third week of January until the February half-term.

- **Spring is in the air.** As everyone returns from half-term, those who are busy wishing their lives away go around saying, 'We're halfway through the year already!' Some aspects of the school may still be difficult, but everyone knows they have broken the back of the year. Unless, of course, the leadership team have planned all the parents' evenings for the term, along with a couple of twilight training sessions, in which case the mood in the staffroom deteriorates as tiredness sets in. (Avoid this scenario.)

- **The clocks change and Easter.** The clocks going forward gradually lifts the mood and with Easter comes a new-found energy. Staff are also buoyed up by the thought of Year 11 leaving soon. They have been ready to go since Christmas and it has been a hard slog.

- **Summer workload.** The weather makes a huge difference during the summer term: it is lovely seeing all your students out on the playing fields (if you are lucky enough to have some outdoor space) looking chilled. Behaviour is definitely better and, in theory, everything should be hunky-dory, but ... how many times during the year did you hear someone say, 'Leave it for now – we'll do that in the summer term when the Year 11s have gone'? Every year, I forget just how hard it can be during the summer term.

Being aware of this continuous cycle won't resolve the issues you encounter, but it will help you and your staff to be more aware of the school year and perhaps become more proactive – for example, pacing yourselves, having realistic expectations and supporting one another.

Always looking at the few

Even at the hardest moments in the most disorganised and chaotic schools, I would estimate that the maximum proportion of students disrupting learning for others is around 10%. In most schools, on most days, almost all the students are in the right place, at the right time, doing the right work. Unfortunately, our eyes are always drawn to poor behaviour because it is what will be commented on by staff or visitors.

When it comes to behaviour in the classroom, the numbers may be slightly different depending on the class you teach. Let's imagine a class where things are not going so well in terms of behaviour and a third of the students are not on task:

Classroom behaviour

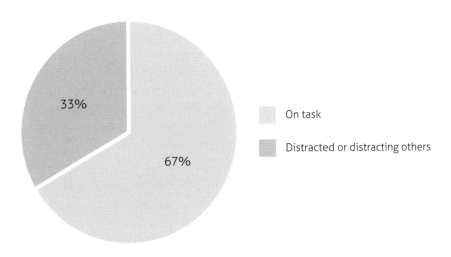

33%

67%

On task

Distracted or distracting others

However, if we analyse the off-task group, most often it will look something like this:

Classroom behaviour

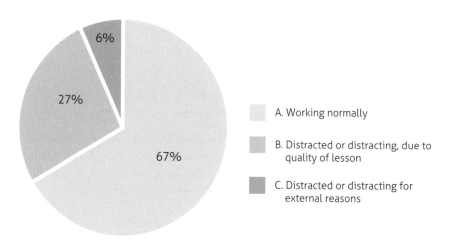

A. Working normally

B. Distracted or distracting, due to quality of lesson

C. Distracted or distracting for external reasons

Most of the students not on task will be as a direct result of what the teacher is doing. For example, is the lesson engaging? Are they challenged? Is the teacher giving regular and meaningful feedback during the lesson? Is the material relevant? This group can swing either way in the lesson, so it is up to the teacher to move them towards group A. What we need to look out for are group B or C students pulling over students from group A into group B.

Group C students are those who have a lot going on in their lives and need additional one-to-one support – although, as the chart above shows, the numbers are very small. Staff must be on the look-out for these students and take some responsibility when things go awry in the classroom. However, if these young people are causing difficulties in every lesson, then they most definitely need additional help. It is the responsibility of the SLT to address this issue.

Even though group C students are small in number, they are a whole-school matter. It isn't that they are unteachable, it is that their needs are far greater than a normal teacher with a class of 30 students can manage effectively. Unfortunately, this links to the fact that cuts in most support agencies, such as social and family support workers, are making it harder for schools to care for their students.

When I talk to teachers about this and bring up their responsibility for group B students, as well as our responsibility as a senior team, the first question I am asked is: 'That's all very well, but what are we doing about these group C students? My teaching is being disrupted.' It is a good question. One of the actions we take on a weekly basis is to highlight the support these students are being given. Staff like to know that something is happening and they feel backed up when they know we are listening. There is excellent additional learning needs (ALN) provision in Wales and special educational needs and disability (SEND) provision in England. Your school may also have a fantastic member of the senior team who is well informed about every external body out there that can help. However, even knowing all this and understanding the figures in the chart above, when something goes wrong in a class or during breaktime, the few students involved suddenly represent the whole school population and murmurs of 'The school's going backwards' start up again.

Staff on a high state of alert

Teaching staff can be triggered into a high state of alert by the handful of students who are causing problems, but this issue tends to be specific to staff who have been or are still experiencing very challenging circumstances. When I first started at Eastern High, the fire alarm went off due to a faulty connection in a radiator. We called the fire brigade who searched the school for over an hour, trying to locate the problem, while we waited outside. Meanwhile, all sort of rumours began, and by the time we were allowed back into the building, social media had done its job. It was already in the local online news, which reported smoke billowing from the school and police, ambulance and fire services in attendance (there was one fire engine). The staff naturally blamed students for the incident, and I was greeted by a host of angry parents when I returned to my office, all telling me that the school was out of control. This was followed up in the evening with calls from councillors, governors and even members of Welsh government.

This was a perfect example of a community on a high state of alert. When staff (and, in this case, the whole community) have gone through a prolonged period of challenge due to a breakdown in school systems or leadership, their fear of returning to that situation remains real for many years afterwards. I still feel it from my time at Hammersmith School, hence my reason for agonising constantly on my abilities to manage behaviour effectively. The staff in my current school certainly still feel it, and so any small incident can spark the fear that leads to them questioning the quality of the school's behaviour management.

It's a school – get real!

I have always made a point of inviting prospective parents to visit the school for a tour at any time. 'In that way,' I tell them, 'you'll see us as we truly are.' It is the best technique for gaining public confidence and reducing a high state of alert. If I can't show them around personally, I always make sure that the SLT member leading the tour mentions at the start that there are over 1,000 young people in the building, which means a thousand sets of adolescent hormones, so things can go wrong at any time. We explain that problems happen in all schools, but that if something does go wrong, we guarantee that it will be dealt with quickly and no one will be left upset for long.

I have to keep reminding myself when I get annoyed or saddened by a behaviour incident that I work in a school; there is going to be trouble from time to time. We can create an ethos and culture for learning that will reduce misbehaviour, but we can never eradicate it. Or can we?

Giving young people the freedom to explore and make mistakes

My wife and I have always allowed our children certain freedoms. There were boundaries, of course, but we didn't want to bring them up under strict control or to be closeted all of the time. We wanted them to learn from their mistakes and gave them a lot of independence. We expected a degree of trust in return and, by and large, it worked. We have lively children, to say the least, but they have thrived on that element of freedom. There are risks attached to this approach, obviously, but they are wiser as a result of their mistakes.

It is the same when you are a head: I don't want quiet, subservient students. I want them to question and be critical when necessary. I want them to tell us where we are getting it wrong. I want them to pursue opportunities. I want them to have certain freedoms around the school and to work out for themselves what is and isn't suitable behaviour. I have already mentioned that we don't have signs up all over the building telling people how they should walk or what areas are out of bounds. I don't want a school where staff are bellowing at the children when they get things wrong at breaktime or during the change-over of classes. We remind them what is and is not appropriate. We trust them to reflect on this and then we expect them to uphold the level of trust they are given.

This doesn't always make for a quiet and perfectly behaved school, but I would like to think that our students are full of life and that they draw lessons from any missteps. A school should be a safe environment, so what better place to learn from your mistakes, socially as well as academically? Not everyone would agree with me, though, which leads me on to my next point.

What we think other people want to see

I like lively environments, but I always have an uneasy feeling that this isn't what other people want to see. Anxiety seems to be a condition of the teaching profession. I am constantly telling staff that they won't be judged negatively if I walk past a noisy classroom. We can all rationalise this: we know that the best learning often comes from animated discourse and interaction. Of course, there is a time for silent work but certainly not continuously. So, why is it we so often revert to type and opt for quiet and orderly rather than giving students the freedom to be expressive?

I remember, during an inspection, that an inspector came in to observe an assembly I was taking. Afterwards, she remarked positively on the content and then said something along the lines of: 'I was really taken aback at the beginning of that assembly. Everywhere in the school there is such a caring, congenial atmosphere. No one shouts and the students are encouraged to take risks in their learning. And then I walk into this assembly and there are staff directing students to seats in an almost aggressive manner, all of them standing at the sides, looming over the students and ready to pounce. It shocked me, to be honest.'

That was another turning point for me. I hadn't even considered this behaviour by staff during assemblies. I just took it for granted: it had been like that in every school in which I had taught. It made me look at not only the way we manage students in assembly but every other aspect of our school too, to ensure we were following our ethos throughout. In assemblies, the teachers should be sitting among the students (unless you are in a school like my current one where there aren't enough seats). And why can't students come in and chat or socialise until we are ready to begin? The test of a good school is whether or not the students settle down when asked to do so at the start of the assembly because they know it is the right thing to do.

We put control mechanisms in place in schools to make it easier for teachers to teach and for senior leaders to get through the day. There is nothing wrong with these measures when they are appropriate. For example, silence is sometimes necessary because we do not want students to disturb the learning of their classmates. However, the rule of insisting on silence when students come into assembly exists because we are afraid of letting go. If young people are going to learn valuable social skills, then we have to loosen up occasionally and give them an opportunity to make mistakes, which we can then put right. A good example, which was a turning point for me, was when I was approached by a student who asked why we had put up a sign telling students they were not allowed to use a lift. He said: 'Sir, if you just tell us in assembly that it isn't appropriate for us to use the lift because it's for disabled people, then we won't use it. If you put that sign up, it just sets up a challenge and some of us are sure to use it.' Behaviour management is fraught with ambiguities.

Cog 3.8: Crime and punishment

So far in this chapter we have looked at how to proactively manage behaviour by deepening our understanding of adolescence and adverse childhood experiences. We have also considered how to foster good working relationships and explored some of the more irrational (but understandable) views we can hold about poor behaviour.

All of this can go a long way to creating a calm school atmosphere, but, as we have seen, a proactive approach won't eradicate all inappropriate behaviour. Young people need boundaries that they learn not to cross and that can give them a sense of security. A system is required. Although I do not intend to present a definitive model, it is difficult to discuss behaviour management and not illustrate good practice.

What follows is the model that we use at Eastern High. Please take any aspect of it, or just the basic concept, and make it your own. We have adapted ideas from other schools and done just that.

A culture for learning and positive relationships policy

We call our behaviour policy a culture for learning and positive relationships policy. We begin with the values and principles that underlie it and then move on to the culture for learning in class and around the school. We divide expectations for behaviour in class into three areas based on a traffic light system (see figure on page 136).

Culture for learning in class

The Eastern promise

How we shine

We strive for excellence.

We respect each other.

We use devices and equipment effectively.

We take pride in our work and our appearance.

Leads to:

Quality work.

Achievement points while you learn.

Outstanding results.

Steps to success

Key habits to improve learning

Arrive on time, coats off.

Come prepared with the equipment for learning.

Stay on task at the set talk level.

Quiet voices that don't interrupt others.

No eating or drinking (water permitted).

Failure to comply leads to:

One warning before teacher sets detention.

Failure to attend detention – you have crossed the red line.

Don't cross the line

No excuse in lessons

Behaviours which prevent learning

Physical or verbal abuse towards others.

Unsafe behaviour.

Leaving class without permission.

Inappropriate use of equipment or digital media.

Behaviour preventing learning from continuing.

Leads to:

Detention of up to one hour.

Any additional sanction decided by the SLT.

Parents will be notified.

The top section is our 'Eastern promise', which highlights the behaviours we want to see. Green points are awarded by teachers which can be exchanged for items in our green reward shop. This doesn't work so well for the older students; however, the green points also count towards our house competition and towards trips and other events, such as cheaper prom tickets. As we will discuss in Cog 4.2, recognition is more important than the reward, so we ensure that recognition is part of our classroom practice and there are frequent celebration assemblies.

The middle box outlines the key habits we want to see from students; in their absence, they can become distracted, divert others or hold up learning. The sanction attached to this is an amber detention. This always follows at least one warning from the teacher and can last up to 20 minutes.

The bottom section means the student has crossed the line. We make it clear that these misdemeanours can be avoided easily and there is no excuse for them. The only red misdemeanour where a student is given a warning first is the one concerning the use of digital devices/media. If a student is caught using a phone without permission, they are asked to put it away. If they argue, they are given a red detention. If they take it out again, they are given a red detention. A red detention lasts between 40 and 60 minutes.

A word on the mechanics of operating this type of system. We brought it in not long after I first took up my post. Teachers had been given some non-negotiable tasks that they had to carry out in each lesson, such as greeting students at the door and ensuring there was a 'do now' activity for students to do when they first entered. When launching the culture for learning to students, we drew their attention to the teachers' non-negotiables to ensure they understood that everyone needs to comply with predetermined behaviours sometimes, adults as well as young people. Staff and students were given the opportunity to contribute to the development of the culture for learning system (and, in the case of parents, comment on it).

We decided to hold detentions centrally rather than relying on the teacher doing it for their own classes (see more on this in the pros and cons on page 138). We also had to work out a system to record and allocate additional sanctions for the students who received multiple amber or red detentions in a day. The system is now online, so parents know instantly if their child has a detention. If they don't wish their child to have it on that day, they can inform us.

We are very clear on when and how staff make duty calls. They should call for a duty member of staff only if learning can no longer continue with the child in the classroom. Staff on duty make an assessment of the situation when they arrive at the class. If the teacher or child is obviously stressed, they will take the student away. However, if the child is in a rational state of mind, the duty member of staff may talk to the student outside and then negotiate a return to the classroom with the teacher. There is a duty room for students to sit in for the remainder of the lesson where they can discuss their behaviour with the duty member of staff and/ or carry on with their classwork.

There is a (non-teaching) member of staff who is responsible for organising the detentions each day, alongside an assistant head who oversees the whole system. Senior and middle leaders are on a rota for running detentions with teachers on a backup rota. We ask teachers who have set red detentions to attend the detention to take part in a restorative session with the student. We chase up any non-attendance to detentions. This has to be relentless in order to ensure that students understand they won't be let off.

The next step in the development of this system is to gradually give detentions back to the teachers, as detentions offer the chance for rebuilding. If a house support officer or head of year notices that a student has received several detentions, they meet with them to discuss the issue after school (the first step to organising a restorative discussion) and then schedule a restorative meeting for the following day, if possible. Alternatively, if your centralised system works, you can insist that all teachers attend detentions to do a quick rebuild, even if it is only for an amber detention.

The pros and cons

There are pros and cons to any system like this. Let's start with the pros:

- It is clear and transparent to all parties. We have tried to avoid any ambiguities.
- It is clear what the reward or sanction will be.
- We know that sanctions are taking place consistently across the school.
- It is quick and easy to apply (see also cons).

- The teacher does not need to stay behind and take the detention or chase up detentions (see also cons).

- It is easy to monitor which teachers are giving out comparatively more sanctions than other teachers.

- Using an online system makes it easy for parents to be kept up to date in real time.

- It is easy to analyse and see who is causing issues across the school.

The cons:

- It is perhaps too quick and easy to give out a sanction.

- It could be perceived as undermining teachers by removing their responsibility for taking detentions, causing the students to lose respect for them.

- It takes time to embed and ensure consistency. (It took us at least three years to identify all the issues and modify procedures to ensure staff were applying the sanctions consistently. We still have to follow up overzealous staff members or those who are obviously struggling but not giving out any sanctions.)

- Initially it can appear difficult to manage; however, it becomes easier as staff buy into the system and it becomes embedded.

Ultimately, we have found that this system gives consistency to students and the staff feel supported. It isn't as cut and dry as a 'three strikes and you're out' type model, which can be too quick-fire and open to abuse. However, it is objective and there isn't much room to debate whether or not the behaviour should be sanctioned. It is true that children need boundaries, and this system provides an appropriate measured response for any child who crosses the line.

Actually, I think our work on relationships and understanding adolescence have been the biggest contributors to transforming behaviour. Our culture for learning system is a backup for when things go wrong, and in my eyes is also a learning tool for students (although they would never agree with me on that one).

In addition to this system, our behaviour policy goes on to provide an outline of expected behaviours for staff, 'what to do if' flowcharts and tips on managing behaviour. I do not describe these approaches in detail here because an authentic, positive ethos will only come about through these issues being discussed with staff and developed together. Our policy also covers other areas which will be discussed in the remainder of this chapter: fixed-term exclusions, bullying, school uniform and social media. I have singled these out because they are common problems for many schools and require a very clear policy. They are also polarising issues and therefore require consultation and discussion with staff and parents.

Cog 3.9: Why fixed-term exclusions don't work

It is all very well having a system in place for those students who don't behave appropriately in class, but what of the repeat offenders, the extreme behaviour incidents and those who cannot cooperate? The students know there will be sanctions and that we will follow them up relentlessly, but they also know that we do everything we can to support them. It goes back to our principle of accepting that as young people they are still developing. Children, especially those who have experienced traumatic events in their lives, need people around them whom they can trust and go to for help when things are difficult. If school staff are *in loco parentis* during the day, then it stands to reason that we should never give up on the young people in our care.

This has big implications for schools. These responsibilities have always been there, but we now know so much more about adolescent development than we did even at the turn of this century, and this makes it all the more imperative that we try to address the needs of our students. Is your school prepared to address these needs? It is hard work and can be costly. In this and the following cog, we will look firstly at alternatives to exclusions and then move on to the levels of intervention a school needs to put in place if it is to be assured that it has tried everything for the child.

Only a week into my first headship, I began to agonise over what to do about the number of fixed-term exclusions the school was giving out. When I had taken on the role, the school had the highest exclusions by far in Bristol, which at the time was the highest excluding local authority in the country. I reasoned, therefore, that the school was likely to be one of the highest excluding schools nationally.

Young people were being excluded on a daily basis, sometimes for 10 days at a time, but I couldn't just dismantle the current system without a suitable replacement in place. As a result, at the end of each day, I would walk out to the gate to say goodbye to the students, only to be met by all the excluded children gathered around, waiting for their friends. They were never abusive; in fact, they were all very jovial as they milled around on their bikes, scooters and skateboards. I got to know a few of the regular gate attenders quite well, who were all very honest with me.

The vast majority of those who had been excluded bore no grudges. They accepted that exclusions were the norm for poor behaviour and quite enjoyed the break from school. Those on longer exclusions didn't enjoy the experience so much, but this was mainly for social reasons rather than the fact that they were missing out on valuable learning experiences. Had I cancelled all fixed-term exclusions at that point, those students who were completely disenfranchised from the education system would have caused the school to spiral downwards even further. On top of that, the staff would have demanded my head on a block, claiming the school was no longer a safe place to work.

There were two things I knew I had to do. The first was to demystify who these young people were. They weren't knife-wielding maniacs or uncontrollable marauding monsters. They were children who had a lot going on in their lives. Now, I know this is often the last (clichéd) thing you want to say to staff who are on high alert and have low morale, but this was the start of me beginning to think about how to peel back and reveal the complex layers of experience and trauma these young people had suffered. I didn't want to do it in order to equip staff with the tools to repair the damage these young people had experienced and turn them all into saviours, but more to raise awareness and instil some empathy in them before they hurled (metaphorically) unruly children from their classrooms.

The second was to find an alternative to exclusions. Around the same time I took up this headship, I was caught on a speed camera and was given the option of either attending a speed awareness course and avoiding having three points on my licence or accepting the three points. I opted for the course. As I sat there during the session, outwardly looking serene while inside I was silently cursing anything and everything, out of the blue I had another little epiphany. I realised that the National Driver Offender Retraining Scheme instructors weren't the evil money-making sons and daughters of Satan I had been led to believe; instead, they were genuinely trying to educate me. Rather than being punished with three points, I had been given the option to learn from my mistakes. (Okay, I had to pay the cost of the fine to be on the course, but let us put that to one side for the moment and focus on the positive.)

We began to develop a similar concept in school. Instead of issuing fixed-term exclusions, we would hold after-school workshops with the aim of educating the students rather than punishing them. The content would relate directly to the misdemeanour – for example, if a child had been fighting, they would be given a session on anger management. We went online and found lots of resources to help us deliver the workshops and developed for ourselves anything we couldn't find.

The basic idea was to have three after-school sessions, each lasting an hour, as an alternative to a one-day exclusion. One member of senior staff and one house support officer would take the workshops each week. On the first evening, the students would each discuss in turn their misdemeanour with one member of staff (while the other set work for any additional students). This would involve exploring in a restorative way what had happened, what they were thinking and how it might have affected others. On the second and third evenings, they continued any work they were doing in relation to the misdemeanour and, in addition (depending on whether or not they were ready to cooperate), take part in any pre-arranged restorative meeting that was necessary.

I have since taken this model to two other schools, and in that time we have had zero fixed-term exclusions. Although, there have been a couple of times when we have had to impose an exclusion for a few days, not as a sanction but to speed up an urgent assessment of the child's needs or while waiting for alternative provision to become available.

From a student point of view, many would have preferred a fixed-term exclusion, but usually by the end of the three days, if the workshops are done well, they have understood the benefits. We have repeat offenders, but they have reduced rapidly in each school, especially when supported by our other interventions.

Most parents have welcomed the strategy. They would prefer their child to be in school where they should be, so they can also see the benefits. As long as the parents of any victims are also made aware of the restorative element to the workshops, they are invariably supportive too.

The staff perspective has been interesting. When we initially set it up, we didn't have the same level of interventions or restorative practices in place, so I would regularly have members of staff coming to me saying, 'I want this child excluded!' This infuriated me, but I soon learned to explain in a calm way why we were holding a workshop and how a restorative meeting would be really conducive to us all moving forwards. In my current school, where all the support systems are well established, in the six years I have been there, not one staff member has come to me demanding an exclusion. They will voice their concerns about a student but never about the system. I am pretty sure this isn't because they live in fear of the SLT but because they understand and believe in the system.

This non-exclusion policy highlights a perfect link between two of the principles we follow: (1) accept that young people are still developing, and (2) give parity to educating and facilitating all aspects of a child's development.

Stages of intervention

When introducing the workshop model, we quickly realised that we would need supporting systems to address a number of issues:

- How we would manage/work with repeat offenders.

- What we would do with those who had committed a very serious offence.

- How we would ensure staff support. (After all, they were the ones possibly facing the student after they had crossed every line in their class the previous day.)

- How we would convince our local authority that an intended permanent exclusion was justified, especially in a school that had previously had a reputation for high exclusion rates. (We will deal with permanent exclusions shortly, but for now it is enough to say that I would never rule out a permanent exclusion.)

Our restorative training began during the initial period of my first headship. We knew that it would have a positive impact; however, it wasn't always enough. Consequently, we began to develop the concept of staged intervention. I took this idea to my next school, where it was fully developed as described below.

There are levels of intervention we can apply when working with young people, depending on the frequency of certain behaviours. If a student does one serious thing wrong, something that is out of character, they should not be treated in the same way as a student who is repeatedly committing misdemeanours. Instead, there needs to be a phased approach.

Stage	Type of behaviours	Possible actions
1	Initial concerns: a few behaviour logs appearing from different subjects.	Monitoring through the tutor. Parents informed.
2	Repeated higher level incidents.	Tutor report in addition to above. Initial discussion with house support officer/head of year.
3	Tutor report has no impact.	Formal referral to head of year/house or equivalent for a report. Internal support (such as mentoring) and external support considered and given where appropriate.
4	Year/house report has no impact and/or repeated dangerous behaviour.	Following extended time at stage 3, referral to internal support centre.[20] Additional external support sought.

....

20 In each school where I have been the head, we have run an internal support centre with approximately 25 students on the cohort at any one time. The students receive a mix of support centre sessions and mainstream classes with support.

Stage	Type of behaviours	Possible actions
5	Support centre not effective and/or repeat behaviour is dangerous or extreme.	External provision: consider using the school's off-site provision. External support continues.
6	No intervention is working.	Consider permanent exclusion or work with local authority to secure specialist school provision.

At each stage there are many actions and referrals we can make. These will be dependent on the school, how it is structured and the level of existing support from MATs, local authorities and other external provision available locally. The point is, before we reach the stage of external exclusion, we should have covered every base and not given up on the child. This process gains the trust of the local authority and any other body that holds you to account with regard to exclusions. As a result, my decision to make a permanent exclusion has never been called into question. We always provide details about what we have tried at each stage and, therefore, it is always taken as a given that we have done everything we possibly can. Parents also appreciate this transparency.

Occasionally, we have to skip stages and place students on a higher stage immediately. This happens when there is an extremely dangerous incident that warrants close supervision. In almost every case, there are underlying external factors that are addressed through this process.

On rare occasions, we have had to move straight to permanent exclusion – for example, for drug dealing – but normally we would try to find an alternative place in another school and organise a negotiated transfer. The bottom line for us is that we only permanently exclude if we think the child's needs would be better served in specialist provision or if the child causes a constant risk to others (or themselves) while in school.

Cog 3.10: What to do about bullying?

Apart from the quality of education, one of the areas that most concerns parents is how happy and safe their child is in the school environment. The main question I am always asked as I show prospective parents around is: 'Is there a lot of bullying here?' My reply is always the same: 'There is bullying in every school in one form or another, just as there is potential bullying in all different settings throughout life.' I then go on to tell parents that what matters most is what schools do to prevent or minimise bullying should it arise and to ensure that everyone in the school community can identify bullying.

When I arrived at Eastern High, it appeared that every upset child was a victim of bullying. The school had already instigated some measures to tackle outbreaks of bullying, but we quickly supplemented these with more education about bullying, the introduction of restorative practices to prevent reoccurrence, systems to ensure better supervision to prevent bullying and mentoring to support vulnerable students (both victims and perpetrators). However, what concerned me most was the school's ability to identify bullying, as this is often neglected.

A bully is now defined as a person who habitually seeks to harm or intimidate those whom they perceive as vulnerable.[21] This often takes place repeatedly and can be found in all walks of life, whether in the workplace, schools or families. The term, initially a form of endearment, began to transform in the mid 17th century to refer to someone who uses strength or influence to harm or intimidate those who are weaker. One of the first examples of this can be seen in 1857 with the publication of Thomas Hughes' novel about life at Rugby School, *Tom Brown's School Days*.[22] Since then, there have been countless studies into the effects and consequences of bullying, how to prevent bullying, how to tackle bullying and how to recognise signs of bullying taking place.

---

21 A Diana Award campaign led to this new definition being accepted by all major dictionaries in 2018 – see https://diana-award.org.uk/news/young-people-bullied-no-longer-weak.
22 Thomas Hughes, *Tom Brown's School Days* (London: Macmillan, 1857).

Few head teachers would ever claim that bullying doesn't exist in their school. If you put over 700 young people together, not to mention more than 100 adults, then relationships are going to break down at times and some people will experience some form of bullying. It seems to be a sad fact of human nature that in any situation, not just in schools, the more powerful will exploit the less powerful, whether it is on the grounds of wealth, status, physical strength or other factors.

As widespread as it may be, the vast majority of schools do well in reducing incidents of bullying. Most schools ensure that students are aware of the range of people they can approach if they are unhappy or experiencing problems. Most school staff are trained to spot signs of bullying among their cohort and know how and when to refer on any concerns. In addition, anti-bullying sessions are normally part of the curriculum and, of course, there are restorative meetings to help prevent reoccurrence.

A great deal of time is put into monitoring and recording incidences of reported bullying, and this is where I begin to have a problem. If I take Eastern High as an example, when we began to improve our bullying prevention systems, the level of reported incidents rose initially. This did not necessarily mean that bullying was getting worse, rather it was easier for students to report it.

We then began to record the number of incidents that were reported as bullying but transpired not to be bullying related. It turned out that it was these non-bullying incidents that were increasing, while actual bullying had levelled out and was now on the decline. Further investigation led us to the conclusion that many students and parents were attaching the label to incidents that were not actually bullying.

This is a sensitive issue. No school wants to discourage students from reporting something that is upsetting them; however, it doesn't help when the term bullying is used inaccurately, as this can often result in the school dealing with the incident in an inappropriate or unhelpful way.

Take this example: a Year 7 student becomes upset because they have fallen out with a long-time friend from primary school. As is often the case, as students make new friends, one child may feel left out as their former friends drift away. Some children may try to cling on to the old friendship and, when rejected, parents naturally become protective of their child's distress. When questioned, the child may find it easier to say they are being bullied than describe the details. By employing a well-used label (albeit unconsciously), the child's distress is given more credibility. The parent, hearing only one side of the story, may also believe their child is being bullied. The friend who has drifted away is not necessarily in the wrong, so pursuing the matter with them will possibly exacerbate the issue. Instead, the distraught child needs reassurance and support in understanding that although the situation is upsetting, they can overcome it, perhaps with some help – for example, by being encouraged to become involved in other activities or develop new interests.

The politics of children's relationships can be complex and easily misinterpreted by both adults and the children themselves. Young people test each other all the time; they test their friends and they test strangers. It is their way of learning about and making sense of social interactions. It is vital therefore that they learn how to cope effectively with clashes of personality and broken relationships. As adults in schools, and as parents, we need to be there to support and enable the children in our care to be strong, but at the same time not to hide their feelings. If they are upset, they should be able to talk about it, so that others can help. However, we must be mindful of the stigma associated with bullying and that using the word bullying prematurely can potentially cloud the real issues.

This can be a difficult viewpoint for some staff and parents to accept, particularly if they have been bullied at school themselves. One way I try to manage parents who come in demanding to see me because their child is being bullied is to bring the conversation around to their own experiences. If it transpires that they were bullied, I try to show understanding about the fears they must have for their child. This often de-escalates the situation and allows for a more rational conversation that isn't muddied by their own experiences and anxieties.

Every case of reported bullying should be taken seriously, but to help us all deal with the situation appropriately, it is essential that we encourage a wider descriptive vocabulary when reporting incidents that are upsetting a young person. It is also important that we establish the facts before we label an incident, asking ourselves questions such as:

- Is the child a victim of deliberate or malicious behaviour?
- Is this behaviour a one-off incident or repeated?
- Is this a case of a falling out between friends?
- Can we do anything to empower the perceived victim?

Thinking carefully before we act is the first step to ensuring that we support the children in our care in the very best way possible. Ultimately, we want to help young people develop healthy relationships. To do so, we need to make sure they are well informed about what bullying actually means.

Cog 3.11: Uniform – a necessity or a source of tension?

Recently, while half listening to the news, my ears pricked up when I heard the words 'headmaster' and 'uniform'. It turned out that an unfortunate head teacher in England was unlucky enough to send some students home for not wearing the correct uniform on a slow news day, and so he hit the headlines. It sparked the usual run of debates across the country: why wear a school uniform? Is a uniform a good thing? Do some schools make unreasonable demands on parents when it comes to the expense of uniforms?

I have debated long and hard with myself as to whether or not I am in favour of uniforms, and the conclusion I have reached is that I am. In the past, I have visited schools in Spain and France, where they don't have uniforms, and I have been envious of the outwardly relaxed atmosphere. The schools may have the same issues to deal with when it comes to working with their students, but there seems to be one less problem to tackle when uniforms don't exist, one less barrier between student and teacher.

In the UK, school staff are continually chasing up students in incorrect uniform. Most of them want to be individual but we try to quash this. As a result, hours of staff time and students' learning time are lost due to lectures from staff, letters sent home, detentions set and meetings with parents. What may have started off as a small matter can sometimes build until eventually parents and governors have to meet. Some schools even exclude.

So, why have school uniforms if they can cause such a headache? There is a strong tradition for uniforms in the UK; we are famous for it. We are still a class-conscious country and an unconscious collective view persists that a collar and tie look smart and are something to which we should aspire. Perhaps this is the reason that white shirts, ties and blazers prevail in the UK. (It is interesting to note that the trend seems to be going in the opposite direction in the workplace.)

Interestingly, in each of the schools I have worked where blazer and tie has been introduced, we consulted the students and parents beforehand and asked them for their preferences: no uniform, branded sweatshirt-type uniform or traditional blazer and tie. The prevalent answer in each school has been for blazer and tie. Consultation is essential if you are planning a change to the uniform.

In my first headship, I dreaded the first day when the students were due to come in wearing the new uniform. My worries were unfounded as they all turned up looking fantastic. If we asked groups of students what they thought, they would all say they loathed the uniform and wanted rid of it. However, when consulted on an individual basis, their comments were more nuanced. They hated putting it on initially, but by the time they were on the way to school and saw other students wearing the same uniform, they realised they looked smart and so began to feel a sense of pride in what they were wearing. I never let them forget how good they look in their uniform.

Those who argue against school uniforms often mention the cost. While I have come across schools with uniforms that are ridiculously expensive and completely impractical, most schools choose affordable branded uniforms that can be bought at a reasonable price from a number of outlets. On this note, it is important to offer cheaper alternatives – for example, an unbranded blazer with the option to sew or iron on the badge. Imagine the cost to parents if faced with children demanding they buy them the latest fashions if uniform didn't exist; a pair of trainers can cost a lot more than the average uniform. Uniform can take the financial pressure away from parents and take the social pressure off students.

Cog 3.12: How concerned should we be about digital and social media?

Never before has a generation so diligently recorded itself accomplishing so little.

Anonymous

I will say from the outset that I am against banning mobile phones in schools. For me, forbidding them would be the easy solution. It would make things more straightforward for teachers and results might even rise. However, this goes against what I believe is the purpose of schools – that is, to educate and prepare young people to function effectively in society and flourish in their adult lives. We need to design schools around the needs of students, not teachers.

Michael Harris's book *The End of Absence* simultaneously grabbed my attention and scared me with its opening sentence: 'Soon enough, nobody will remember life before the Internet.'[23] I think about it often as I plead with my daughters to close down whatever social media platform they are hooked on at that moment, or when I ask them how they can study for exams while listening to music through headphones. I must also confess that in the time it has taken me to write these two paragraphs, I have picked up my phone and put it back down again twice, successfully managing to stave off the temptation to open it and check on all the latest information I don't really need right now.

Okay, so I have admitted that I am failing as a father when it comes to helping my daughters manage their digital devices, and I am also pretty useless as an individual in terms of self-control, so how can I possibly hope to do any better as a head teacher? For the past 10 years or so, it has become harder with each passing

---

23 Michael Harris, *The End of Absence: Reclaiming What We've Lost in a World of Constant Connection* (New York: Penguin, 2015), p. 7.

month, or even week, and I become increasingly alarmed at how little we are doing to address the digital tidal wave that is sweeping over us.

Yuval Noah Harari's *Sapiens* is a book about the history of the development of Homo sapiens.[24] In it, he describes how as humans transitioned from being hunter-gatherers to farmers during the agricultural revolution, there could well have been a point when humans suddenly stopped in their tracks and said, 'My God, what have we done?' Technology had advanced, but at what cost? Longer working hours; more disease, wars and dictators; rules that restrained; less time for creativity and leisure.

The world is now in the midst of a digital information and communication revolution. Just as farming brought huge benefits to the human race, so digital media is bringing huge benefits in terms of ease of access to information and making many aspects of our lives more convenient. However, just as farming also brought many disadvantages, so too does digital media: chronic eye strain, sleep disturbance, wasted hours, online harassment (much easier than the old face-to-face approach) and identity theft, among many others. An acknowledgement of this demands that we give much more time and thought to educating the inheritors of this revolution.

As schools, we have a responsibility to focus on those aspects of life and society that have a major influence on the quality of our lives – positive and negative. We do it with literacy and numeracy and with wider subject areas such as science, so can we do it in relation to the use of digital media?

We can divide the inappropriate use of digital media in the context of our educational responsibilities into four areas: misuse in the classroom, accessing inappropriate or illegal sites, procrastination and time spent on a device, and malicious or damaging comments. The final three can occur in or out of school when the student is alone or with their peers.

Misuse in the classroom

Educating young people to use digital media appropriately in the classroom should be embedded into the school ethos. It is about how we model good

---

24 Yuval N. Harari, *Sapiens: A Brief History of Humankind* (London: Harvill Secker, 2014).

practice and the extent to which we allow young people to make mistakes, but it is also about being there to educate if it goes wrong. This could take the form of educational workshops to follow up any misdemeanour or, at the other end of the spectrum, sanctions to remind the student what is and is not acceptable.

As we saw earlier in this chapter, when describing our culture for learning, one easy solution is to allow students to have their phones in school switched on but in silent mode. If a student takes it out without permission in a lesson, they are asked to put it away. If they argue, there is an automatic sanction (an after-school detention). If they put it away without arguing, but take it out again later in the lesson, there is another automatic sanction. It is a pretty crude way to move students towards good habits but it works. Little by little, they begin to understand when it is acceptable to use their phones.

Over time, this constant drip-feed of educational workshops and sanctions will help young people to develop better and more fitting habits in school and their future workplace. However, what it doesn't do is tackle inappropriate use when they are with peers or by themselves.

Accessing inappropriate or illegal sites

As a nation, we half-heartedly educate young people in many areas that can have a significant impact on their lives, such as mental and physical health, drugs and alcohol, relationships and sex, and careers education. Unfortunately, personal, social, health and economic (PSHE) education can tend to be an add-on in schools and not given the same status as major subjects – and right at the end of the topics queuing up to have a place on the PSHE curriculum is the appropriate use of digital media.

How much time do we spend in classrooms discussing the morality of the websites that some young people access? Do we give students opportunities to make mistakes in school by accessing unsuitable sites and then discussing the content with them? We teach students how to use information and communications technology and we do some education around safe use, but even this is sparsely taught as a topic. If I were to sum up the teaching of e-safety in schools across Britain, it would be: 'We've done "safety on the internet" for this year – tick! Now let's move on to something else.'

Rather than allowing safe use to be embedded into all our practices, we spend a lot of money locking everything down by using good filtering systems. Wouldn't it be far more effective to allow open access to all websites in schools and instead spend the money on very efficient monitoring systems which would pick up on students viewing harmful or offensive material? This would open up opportunities for school staff to discuss (and, if necessary, apply sanctions) the inappropriateness of certain sites, the dangers of giving away personal information or, just as importantly, procrastination.

The trouble is, I am not sure that parents would agree to their child having open access to the internet in school. Schools would have to be 100% confident that they could track everything. But, looking at it another way, isn't it better that this happens in school, which is a relatively safe environment where unsafe browsing can be picked up on and discussed – that is, real-time education? This is far more preferable to a child gaining access in an unmonitored environment (which may happen at home) where they won't get this education.

The same principles apply to inappropriate use, such as being on a game during a lesson or study time. If we simply ban our children from using mobiles and tablets, we only postpone the inevitable day when they are at work with no good habits or skills to resist the dopamine-fuelled rush which can occur when they open a new screen. Part of this education has to include self-monitoring and regulation, so that young people can develop positive behaviours and self-control. Take the device away and all they are left with are dire warnings ringing in their ears, which over time can turn into a meaningless drone.

Procrastination and time spent on a device

A survey by Ofcom found that, on average, children between the ages of 5 and 15 spend two hours and 11 minutes per day online and one hour and 52 minutes a day watching TV.[25] To me, this highlights the extent to which I am failing as a parent because my three children spend more time than that online, although they watch less TV.

---

25 Ofcom, 'Why Children Spend Time Online' (4 February 2019). Available at: https://www.ofcom.org.uk/about-ofcom/latest/features-and-news/why-children-spend-time-online.

According to the Royal College of Paediatrics and Child Health, there is essentially 'no evidence' that screen use is 'toxic' to health.[26] However, they do identify indirect effects such as a loss of sleep and the resultant loss of concentration, the fact that it detracts from doing other constructive or physical activities, and the obvious dangers associated with unsupervised online time. This isn't necessarily just a digital issue; procrastination can take many forms. However, it is about recognising that online activity, with its accompanying dopamine rush, can be a major source of distraction.

In schools, this requires constant dialogue and forums where students can discuss the amount of time they spend on the internet. I am also a huge fan of project-based learning, one of the benefits of which is that it allows good habits to develop. For example, setting milestones in projects and being strict about deadlines helps students to train themselves to avoid time-wasting. This is such a hard problem to overcome, and I feel like a hypocrite writing about it, because I know I will be distracted by something in the next 10 minutes!

Malicious or damaging comments

Rarely a week goes by when a politician or someone in the public eye isn't vilified for posting something tactless (or worse) online or is caught on camera texting when they should be engaged in their work. Photos don't stay private, every social media post is recorded forever and stories are exaggerated with every new Tweet.

Studies have been done on the number of young people rejected from job interviews due to the content of their social media profile – almost one in five according to YouGov.[27] Another survey claims that over a third of employers have reprimanded or fired a member of staff because of online content.[28] In addition, I would estimate that, without exaggeration, well over 80% of fallings-out, arguments and fights in schools are due to what someone has said about someone else on a social

---

26 See https://www.rcpch.ac.uk/resources/health-impacts-screen-time-guide-clinicians-parents.
27 Matthew Smith, 'Disgracebook: One in Five Employers Have Turned Down a Candidate Because of Social Media', *YouGov* (10 April 2017). Available at: https://yougov.co.uk/topics/politics/articles-reports/2017/04/10/disgracebook-one-five-employers-have-turned-down-c.
28 Jane Burnett, 'Survey: 34% of Employers Reprimanded or Fired Someone Over Online Content', *The Ladders* (15 August 2018). Available at: https://www.theladders.com/career-advice/survey-34-of-companies-reprimanded-or-fired-an-employee-over-online-content.

network. Speaking to other head teachers, this problem is widespread and increasing.

In *The 5 Second Rule*, Mel Robbins advocates acting on an idea or intention within five seconds before the brain sabotages it with over-thinking.[29] This inspired me to wonder whether we can harness the five-second pause with respect to our use of digital media. We consulted with staff and students and came up with three situations in which we need to take a five-second pause before continuing: before picking up and using a digital device, before opening a message or website, and before pressing the send or post button. We then asked staff, students and parents for their opinions on what we ought to think about during the five-second pause.

As a result of these soundings, we came up with a set of Five-Second I-Rules:

● Before picking up and using a digital device, take five seconds to consider:

  › Am I putting off doing something more important or worthwhile?

  › Is this an appropriate time to use the device (e.g. it might be unacceptable during lessons, work hours or at the family dinner table)?

  › Am I permitted to use this device? (Is it mine?)

  › Am I using my own log-in or am I using someone else's password to cause mischief?

● Before opening or looking closely at any message or website, take five seconds to consider:

  › Do I know and/or trust the sender? (Could the message or site spread a virus? Am I safe?)

  › Does it look like it should be reported? (Is it potentially against the law or dangerous?)

  › Should I discuss anything that upsets or worries me with my parents or school?

  › Is the site appropriate? (Is it unlawful, wrong, unethical or exploitative? Will I get into trouble using it? Is it age appropriate?)

● Before pressing the send or post button, take five seconds to consider:

  › Is what I have written factual? (Am I spreading gossip or rumour? Is what I have written slanderous?)

29 Mel Robbins, *The 5 Second Rule: The Fastest Way to Change Your Life* (New York: Savio Republic, 2017).

> Is what I am sending within the law (e.g. hateful, inciting racism, child pornography)?

> Is what I am sending harmful or upsetting to others?

> Will what I am sending harm me now or in the future? (What will current or future partners and/or employers think?)

These are just some of the thoughts we all need to consider before we commit to any of these actions. I say 'we' because all of us ought to do this. There are other ways to procrastinate, such as making a cup of tea, tidying up and so on, but nothing draws you in like digital media. And whereas making a cup of tea or tidying up will have an end point, digital time-wasting can be endless.

We also all need to get involved with the Five-Second I-Rules because we can't do it alone, especially young people. I am certainly not in the habit of doing this and only occasionally remember, so I need help from others around me. We all need to remind each other to apply the five-second rule until it becomes habit-forming. At school, we need to be talking about it all the time until it is well and truly fixed in all of our heads. We also need to encourage parents to do the same.

What to take from this chapter

Relationships come first in schools. Listening to young people and making the time and effort to understand them will enhance the quality of your teaching, not only in terms of student learning but also the well-being of staff. To understand young people, fully invest in exploring theories relating to infant mental health, adolescent brain development, attachment theory and adverse childhood experiences. Then ask yourself:

● Why are the first two years crucial, and what relevance does this have to me (even as a secondary school teacher)?

● Why do my adolescent students take risks, challenge and behave in unpredictable ways?

● What impact do these theories have in my classes?

This will help you to discover effective and appropriate ways to develop healthy relationship templates through:

- Making and maintaining positive relationships with your students – learning to show that you are there to support them to learn with unconditional respect.

- Managing relationships when they begin to break down. When you feel yourself moving into the red zone, try to remember that they are young people who are still developing emotionally. They will make mistakes and errors of judgement.

- Mending or moving on relationships when they begin to break down. Apply restorative approaches where appropriate.

Overall, remember to be patient. The utopia described above doesn't happen overnight. All young people need boundaries; what is important is how you help them to avoid crossing lines and how you respond when they do.

Chapter 4

An Ethos of Belonging and Inclusiveness

A child's and adolescent's functioning in school is inextricably linked with his or her sense of belonging and connection to the school environment and his or her relationships with peers and teachers within it.

Kimberly Schonert-Reichl[1]

My current two-year-old school building is designed to last for 40 years or more. While we were designing it, the question I kept asking myself and others involved in the build was this: is there really going to be a need for schools as we know them in 40 years' time?

It was interesting yet worrying to read that in March 2018, the number of home-educated children had doubled in the previous four years. In the UK that amounts to 52,770 children being educated at home, sometimes by parents or a collective of parents.[2] In the United States, there are around 2.5 million children being home-educated and the figure is growing annually at a rate of 2–8%.[3] There is still no compulsory register for home-schooled children, so this may be the tip of the iceberg.

In addition, during the COVID-19 pandemic, many more parents have been forced to home-educate their children due to school closures. When the situation returns to normal, how many of these parents – who may have settled into a routine with their children – will choose to send them back? In the first eight months of the

---

1 Kimberly Schonert-Reichl, 'Children and Youth at Risk: Some Conceptual Considerations'. Paper prepared for the Pan-Canadian Education Research Agenda Symposium, Ottawa, 6–7 April 2020, p. 9. Available at: https://www.researchgate.net/profile/Kimberly-Schonert-Reichl/publication/237308266_Children_and_Youth_at_Risk_Some_Conceptual_Considerations/links/00b7d526f0df311b49000000/Children-and-Youth-at-Risk-Some-Conceptual-Considerations.pdf.
2 David Foster and Shadi Danechi, *Home Education in England*. House of Commons Library Briefing Paper No. 5108 (2019), p. 16. Available at: https://commonslibrary.parliament.uk/research-briefings/sn05108.
3 Brian D. Ray, 'Homeschooling: The Research', *National Home Education Research Institute* (3 May 2020). Available at: https://www.nheri.org/research-facts-on-homeschooling.

academic year 2020/2021 there was a 75% rise in the number of parents home-educating their children,[4] with some local authorities reporting a 200% rise in the number of parents wishing to withdraw their child from school and home-educate.[5] The drive towards a blended learning approach and the creation of more online learning resources continues to make it easier for parents to home-educate their children, especially more affluent, middle-class families. I worry about the effect this may have on the class divide.

How does all of this affect our school ethos? It reveals that some sections of the community are no longer reliant on schools. The education on offer, and even the ethos of the school and its practices, are not enough for the parents of children in the local area. This lack of confidence in the capacity of schools to meet the needs of the vast majority of children may result in growing numbers of parents resorting to homeschooling. Most importantly, this shift in parents' perceptions and young people's own experiences may lead them to develop the belief that schools are not as relevant to their future lives as they might have been once. Resultant behaviours may range from a decline in motivation and drive to study in school to a refusal to cooperate or defiance at having to attend by law.

As we will see in this chapter, schools can and should offer much more than a subject-led curriculum. This wider scope of education is evident when we consider the four areas of sustainability described in Cog 2.6, but the extended nature of schooling becomes even clearer when we look at a recent example of a nation that is developing a new curriculum. The four purposes of the new curriculum for Wales, as set out in the Donaldson Review, include:

- ambitious, capable learners, ready to learn throughout their lives

- enterprising, creative contributors, ready to play a full part in life and work

- ethical, informed citizens of Wales and the world

- healthy, confident individuals, ready to lead fulfilling lives as valued members of society.[6]

---

4   Alix Hattenstone and Eleanor Lawrie, 'Covid: Home-Education Numbers Rise by 75%', *BBC News* (19 July 2021). Available at: https://www.bbc.co.uk/news/education-57255380.
5   Freddie Whittaker, 'Investigation: Minister Intervenes As Home Education Soars', *Schools Week* (23 October 2020). Available at: https://schoolsweek.co.uk/investigation-minister-intervenes-as-home-education-soars.
6   Graham Donaldson, *Successful Futures: Independent Review of Curriculum and Assessment Arrangements in Wales* [Donaldson Review] (2015), p. 29. Available at: https://gov.wales/sites/default/files/publications/2018-03/successful-futures.pdf.

Under both frameworks, the main beneficiaries of schools are not only the students but also the communities they serve. There is a symbiotic relationship between the school, its students and the local community, which can play a major role in contributing to the success of the school.

As we move further into the 21st century, this expanded concept of schooling is essential if we are to enable young people to flourish in life. Encouraging a sense of belonging will not only engage students (which is vital) but will also encourage the community to continue using their local school and contribute towards its vision. This requires community buy-in – that is, confidence, belief and pride in their local school. Without it, a school will begin to decline and possibly local confidence and aspiration with it. Creating a sense of belonging, then, is another key ingredient to the formation of a healthy school ethos and should involve both students and the wider community.

In this chapter we will explore the nature and concept of belonging, the importance this has in relation to school ethos and how a sense of belonging might be created. We will do this in the following way:

- Cog 4.1 begins by acknowledging that schools must work in partnership with the community it serves, if it is to create a sense of belonging for its students. To ensure full engagement and cooperation, the school has to address the concerns of the local population. This will make an obvious contribution to the whole-school ethos. Exploring this cog will better equip you to answer the following questions:

  › What are the main concerns parents have with regard to schooling?

  › How can we ensure that all parents know about the positive aspects of our school curriculum offer? And if they do, to what extent do they buy into it?

  › If our school was to suddenly close for good, what impact would it have on the local community?

- Cogs 4.2 and 4.3 consider the practices and activities we might undertake in schools to create a sense of belonging among our students, and then go on to examine some of the blocks and how we might overcome them. These cogs will help you to answer the following questions:

  › What are the key elements to creating a sense of belonging in our school?

> How will we know if our students feel they have some ownership of the school?

> How can we prevent or reduce the impact of some of the blocks that may arise?

● Cogs 4.4 and 4.5 widen the scope of belonging to take in staff and the wider community, exploring why it is important to create a sense of belonging for the school among these two groups and how this, in turn, will deepen the sense of belonging young people feel for their school. Exploring these cogs will enable you to answer the following questions:

> What can I do to create a genuine sense of belonging among staff in our school?

> How can I manage underperformance but maintain a sense of belonging among staff?

> How can our school broaden its influence so that stakeholders in the community feel a sense of belonging with the school community?

● Cogs 4.6 and 4.7 examine two particular aspects of the school relating to inclusion, diversity and equality. We can create a sense of belonging in our schools but do we include everyone? Exploring these cogs will help you to answer the following questions:

> How does our school ensure that every student can participate in every facet of school life?

> How do we personalise but avoid segregation?

> How authentic is the celebration of diversity in our school?

Cog 4.1: A sense of belonging begins with community buy-in

As we begin to create a sense of belonging in schools, we must consider community concerns and needs as much as we do the concerns and needs of students. If we are to maintain a school ethos that is positive, vibrant and supportive, it is essential that as school leaders we make every effort to understand why some parents in the locality may be disgruntled with their local school or schools in general.

Some of the main reasons behind the rising figures for homeschooling, as outlined in a House of Commons Briefing Paper, are listed below,[7] followed by some potential solutions to these issues. In the rest of this chapter, we will go on to consider a more holistic approach to these matters.

1. Dissatisfaction with the school or school system

Many parents are unhappy with the quality of education provided in their child's school. Some believe their child would receive a better education at home or with a small group of like-minded parents. (This was one of the reasons why legislation was passed in 2010 for groups of parents to set up free schools in England.)

Possible ways to address this include:

- Make the curriculum clear and easy to understand for all, ensuring that programmes of studies for the term ahead are published on the school website and publicised to parents. Invite parents in for subject-specific information evenings where they can learn more about the curriculum, ask questions or raise concerns.

---

7   Foster and Danechi, *Home Education in England*, pp. 4–5.

● Make parents aware of all your quality assurance procedures. Parents will feel reassured to know that your school carries out regular lesson observations, scrutinises the quality of student work and teacher assessment in books, and works closely with other schools to moderate standards.

2. Ideological or philosophical views and religious or cultural beliefs

Social media, among other factors, is undoubtedly pushing us towards a world more polarised in its views. Religion, environment, race, gender, political ideology; there are extreme views out there about identity politics which social media exacerbates. Many people seem happy to dive headlong into one camp or the other without really looking at the facts or implications.

Putting aside the bigger national and global examples of polarisation and extremism, schools also face these issues at a local level. For example, the installation (or non-installation) of gender-neutral toilets is a potential tinder box that schools may have to contend with if they don't want to lose the support of parents. It is a topic that has led to some very public protests. The Department for Education's 2019 policy regarding relationships and sex education is another example where parents are threatening to remove their children (especially those of primary age) from school.[8]

Cultural and ideological controversies like these may increasingly lead parents to withdraw their children, especially if they feel the school is not supporting their firmly held beliefs. It is now much easier to home-educate – and social media channels provide a supporting network, as well as educational resources. There may even be enough parents with similar views in the local area to run small, shared tutorial groups or even apply to open a free school.

Possible ways to address this include:

● Refer back to Chapter 1 and ensure that the vision and underpinning principles of your school are clear. A robust rationale for your vision will

8   Department for Education, *Relationships Education, Relationships and Sex Education (RSE) and Health Education: Statutory Guidance for Governing Bodies, Proprietors, Head Teachers, Principals, Senior Leadership Teams, Teachers* (2019; updated July 2020). Available at: https://www.gov.uk/government/publications/relationships-education-relationships-and-sex-education-rse-and-health-education.

provide clarity and transparency for the community. This needs to be revisited regularly with parents through parent forums and the governors' annual report to parents. (If your governors don't produce a report for parents, the school ought to produce its own covering all aspects of school life and achievements from the previous year.)

- Carry out regular surveys and consultations with parents regarding any new policy that will directly influence their child's education. For example, during the COVID-19 pandemic, our school consulted with parents on whether or not to make mask-wearing compulsory for all students. We did this via surveys and online forums. The Welsh government had advised that schools in new buildings may wish to consider their own circumstances and risk assess accordingly. We explained to parents that the school operates in a brand new building with a good ventilation system. The parents supported our move not to make masks mandatory anywhere in the school. Throughout the periods when the school was open, we constantly kept in touch with parents through live online updates and weekly newsletters, and they supported us throughout.

3. Special educational needs provision

In the UK, as many as one in five children being home-educated have special educational needs and disabilities. This may be due in part to local authorities reporting a £500 million funding gap for children with SEND.[9] Parents are becoming increasingly frustrated that their child is not being properly supported in school and so many decide to take on the responsibility for educating their child.

Due to the UK government's austerity programme and the growth in young people being diagnosed with various additional learning needs, schools are having to reinvent themselves in order to meet their students' requirements. This can be difficult and there are suggestions that schools are coercing parents to remove their children from school – a practice known as 'off-rolling'.[10]

9   May Bulman, 'Children "Falling Off the Grid" in the Tens of Thousands Amid Surge in Pupils Leaving Mainstream Education', *The Independent* (3 February 2019). Available at: https://www.independent.co.uk/news/uk/home-news/home-schooling-education-children-commissioner-anne-longfield-a8760951.html.
10 Richard Adams, 'Schools Pushing Children into Home Schooling Say Councils', *The Guardian* (17 January 2019). Available at: https://www.theguardian.com/education/2019/jan/17/schools-pushing-children-into-home-schooling-say-councils.

Possible ways to address this include:

- A clear grouping or setting policy that highlights the personalised approach the school is taking. (Cog 4.6 describes this in more detail.)

- Working closely with the local authority to ensure a more consistent approach among schools to meet the needs of all young people. One school working alone is not enough.

4. Bullying

Bullying has always been a major concern for parents, so there are many groups and organisations available to help parents organise homeschooling if their child is being bullied. Safety is another crucial issue. In the urban schools in which I have worked, we have worked closely with parents who report fears for their child's safety not only to and from school but also in school. They are also worried about the rise in knife crime and the ubiquitous drug problems (which is now extending into rural areas too).

Possible ways to address this include:

- Develop a strong, positive ethos and culture for learning as described in this book.

- Develop and then publicise to parents the working relationships the school has with external organisations, such as the police, children's services, relevant charities and sporting bodies.

5. Health reasons, particularly mental health

The incidence of mental health conditions among adolescents is rising rapidly, and alongside it the anxiety it causes for parents.[11] The extent to which this is a 21st-century phenomenon caused by 21st-century factors (e.g. social media), or whether this is due to a rise in presentation and diagnosis, is not the main focus for us here. Rather, it is the numbers that are a cause for concern.

11 David Gunnell, Judi Kidger and Hamish Elvidge, 'Adolescent Mental Health in Crisis', *BMJ* 361 (2018): k2608. DOI:10.1136/bmj.k2608

In addition, although schools are becoming increasingly trauma informed and are developing systems and structures to deal with trauma, parents – who are just as well informed – are looking for alternatives to ensure their child is looked after appropriately. Mainstream schooling may not be the answer for these parents.

Possible ways to address this include:

- As with all of the concerns described above, a close working partnership with parents is essential, alongside a strong tutor or pastoral system (as described in Cogs 3.4 and 4.2), which is forever watchful and responsive to students' needs.

It is clear that schools are in danger of trying to fill a bottomless hole by attempting to deal with every student's needs. Schools need to be mindful of this problem and work within their capacity: being transparent about what you can and can't address and being clear about the effectiveness of any interventions or systems you put in place. Schools also need to build resilience in parents by working with them to find coping mechanisms.

Parents are open to much conflicting information through social media and the media in general, to the extent that their protective instinct comes to the fore. This can often result in the reactive measure to withdraw their child from school. In my own experience, when an application to homeschool comes through from a parent, it is often too late to change their mind. This is why close, regular communication via the child's tutor is crucial.

School closures and online learning

School closures is not an area covered in the House of Commons briefing paper; however, as mentioned at the beginning of this chapter, during the coronavirus outbreak a fear developed among some parents about sending their children back to school following closures. Alternatively, having become accustomed to teaching their children at home, many decided that homeschooling was the better option. COVID-19 may have provided the push that certain parents required, especially if they gained in confidence or joined a home–school support group. Although continued homeschooling will depend on working practices, many people may continue to work from home and will keep their school-aged children at home with them.

That said, there is one stand-out reason behind the growing phenomenon of homeschooling, and that is the ease with which parents can find online support, ranging from advice and support groups to resources and online schooling. It is a lot easier to home-educate your child today than it was even 10 years ago. The growth of online learning and the ease of accessing materials, which has led to virtual classrooms and organisations such as the Khan Academy, has no doubt influenced parents' decisions about home education. Many of you will have watched Sugata Mitra's TED Talk 'Build a School in the Cloud' (if not, watch it now!),[12] which highlights the power (and lure) of cloud-based learning. In short, it has become easier for dissatisfied parents to home-educate their children.

This leads me to believe that, in the future, regular school attendance may decline. Parents who are bombarded on a daily basis with all the potential horrors the world can throw at their children will increasingly question the wisdom of sending them to school, while young people themselves will begin to question the need to be present in a physical building. Why would they when they know how and where to find the answers at the touch of a button?

Cog 4.2: Creating a sense of belonging for young people

If schools are to be successful in maintaining their relevance for young people, they must first motivate and encourage their students to continue attending. When it comes to attendance, we tend to think of those who require the most encouragement as being the low-attaining, often vulnerable learners, possibly from disadvantaged backgrounds. In fact, we need to widen our remit to all young people, including high-attaining students from more affluent backgrounds whose

12 Sugata Mitra, 'Build a School in the Cloud' [video], *TED.com* (February 2013). Available at: https://www.ted.com/talks/sugata_mitra_build_a_school_in_the_cloud?language=en.

parents are most likely to spearhead a new pattern of non-attendance – for reasons hitherto not yet considered by schools.

Belonging is about acceptance and affinity. It is a human necessity, just like our need for food and shelter. It is 'Such a simple word for [a] huge concept.'[13] In the journey towards creating a sense of belonging for our students, schools should aim to adopt the following six practices.

1. Offer a relevant, agile curriculum, planned in partnership with the school community

Schools must not be regarded solely as environments where students come to learn about specific aspects of our world as outlined in a preordained curriculum. The curriculum should be meaningful to the young people who attend, building relevance into everything they do, focusing on local issues where possible and developing outwards to consider regional, national and global matters. Curriculum content needs to be flexible, but always problem solving or enquiry based in order to develop real-life skills and dispositions which will stay with young people throughout their lives.

If we are to fully engage students, they need to be more involved, not only through participating in learning activities that are relevant to their lives, but also through having a say (to some extent) on curriculum content. Many countries are bound by a national curriculum, but there is some space to expand or introduce new topics, especially for non-exam year groups. Ideally, students should have opportunities to explore and discuss significant issues in depth which will motivate them to study and learn. Framing this within genuine problem-solving situations and creative or entrepreneurial ventures will further strengthen their motivation.

---

13 Karyn Hall, 'Create a Sense of Belonging', *Psychology Today* (24 March 2014). Available at: https://www.psychologytoday.com/gb/blog/pieces-mind/201403/create-sense-belonging.

2. Provide a safe haven where young people have the opportunity to reflect on their own lives, learn from mistakes and develop a risk-sensible approach to life

I would love to introduce into my school a timetable similar to the one I referred to in Cog 2.3, where scheduled lessons mainly take place in the morning and then in the afternoon, most students work from home (apart from practical subjects) and teachers have the time to thoroughly mark students' work and run tutorials during which they provide quality feedback.

The discussions we had concerning implementation always returned to the possible antisocial or dangerous situations in which some students might find themselves, particularly the vulnerable individuals. The detractors were always forgetting that we send our students off for six weeks every summer to do as they please in their local communities.

For me, this revealed something about a hidden purpose of schooling: childcare. I agree that parents and schools shouldn't allow young people to go unsupervised for too long without any structure. However, schools are not institutions of social control and nor are they a babysitting service. We must explore ways to ensure that these hidden purposes are incidental to the work we do, rather than directing school systems and curriculum content.

Certainly, childcare is an issue for primary-age students, but at secondary schools it is possible to be more flexible in the organisation of the school day. However, for this to work, we need to create learning environments where students want to come and learn together with their peers, where they are given time and space to reflect on and make sense of the issues going on in their own lives.

Of course, young people make mistakes when they are out of school, but we need to devote more time to allowing them to learn from these mistakes in school. Many would argue that the world is a more dangerous place than it ever has been. If so, then surely the time is right to train young people to cope with these dangers in a resilient and capable way. We should be helping them to develop risk-sensible rather than risk-averse or risk-reckless behaviours.

3. Foster healthy relationships in a welcoming, supportive and caring environment

An essential ingredient to creating a sense of belonging is the degree to which schools foster healthy and vibrant relationships between student and student, students and staff, school and parents, and school and local community. This must be a priority. It is about students feeling welcomed, cared for and supported. The 5M's mentioned in the previous chapter is an example of how we can achieve this.

4. Develop a high-quality pastoral system

An excellent pastoral system is an obvious prerequisite when it comes to creating a sense of belonging. I include it here to highlight the fact that we already do this well in schools and it plays a vital part in preparing young people for the challenges they will face in the 21st century. Developing a school fit for the future is certainly not a case of out with the old and in with the new.

We have welcomed Spanish visitors to our school on two separate occasions. They spent their time observing lessons and following groups of students. On both occasions, they were really impressed with three aspects of the school: assemblies, our tutor groups and house system, and the additional support on offer (e.g. teaching assistants, mentors/heads of house, child protection officer). None of this is very different from any other school in the UK – we tend to take them for granted – but they are vital to the life of the school. I would argue that they are also essential to the local community. Sometimes it is worth taking a step back and looking at what is working well in your school through another pair of eyes.

Assemblies

Assemblies create an atmosphere of collective community where ideas can be shared and beliefs and values explored. They bring people together to participate in a way that is happening less and less in society. They communicate a common purpose, provide security and help give young people a sense of direction. I like to see assemblies taking place in school as often as possible. If nothing else, the students get to see the whole picture and feel part of something, even if only unconsciously.

Assemblies used solely to call out bad behaviour or repeat school rules can result in a negative environment, which can turn them against the community. For this reason, such injunctions should be used sparingly. However, they can also serve a purpose in letting everyone know that there are codes of conduct to which every community member must adhere if it is to function effectively. Almost all young people want structure and reassurance with regard to their well-being and safety, and so they will appreciate these types of assembly too.

Tutor groups and the house system

Cog 3.4 describes our vertically organised learning families. Like assemblies, these create a bond among the students, with the older students supporting and looking out for the younger ones. When we first set up the family system, the students reported that it felt artificial to be brought together with other children of different ages; normally they wouldn't dream of mixing. Over time, meeting twice a day (40 minutes in total) has created a real sense of belonging.

Each learning family sits within one of four houses (another British institution of which the Spanish teachers had no experience until I mentioned Harry Potter!). The houses are a vehicle for competitions and create a feeling of identity, as well as reinforcing the sense of belonging we are trying to foster.

During the COVID-19 pandemic, when our school was closed, we maintained a very good attendance rate compared to many other schools, mainly due to the house systems and learning families. The highest attended online session was always learning family time. It was here that we maintained a sense of belonging, which in turn encouraged students to attend their online subject sessions.

Pastoral support staff

Working in a school in a deprived area can place enormous demands on the pastoral support system. In the past decade, schools have not only seen cuts in their own budgets but have had to contend with cutbacks in the many support services and charities which once provided additional assistance. As a consequence, schools have had to reinvent themselves to cope not only with the lack of external support but also with the rising numbers of young people in need. As mentioned in Cog 4.1, these numbers are likely to be exacerbated by the greater awareness of mental health conditions, leading to higher numbers of children being diagnosed. The forward-thinking school that works closely with its community will also have to consider the support it can provide to parents.

Our school offers an excellent level of pastoral support to students and parents through various staff appointments – for example, attendance officer, child protection officer, family liaison officer, mentors, off-site alternative provision, trauma and vulnerable student carers. This level of support is not easy to achieve and involves intensive budgetary prioritisation in respect of pastoral staff versus teaching staff.

It often feels as if there is a never-ending demand to meet new and emerging needs. While a good tutor system can lessen the pressure on school budgets for additional pastoral staff, it can only manage for so long before things become unmanageable. Schools cannot hope to survive in isolation. They need to build collaborative working relationships with other schools with whom resources and costs can be shared, and develop partnerships with external agencies, charities and local church groups.

If the comments made by our Spanish visitors are anything to go by, the UK is a step ahead when it comes to creating a sense of belonging. However, in our financially straitened and time-poor world, it would be remiss of us to neglect the significance that these three aspects of schooling play in developing and maintaining a positive school ethos.

5. Student voice

I have referred to student voice several times throughout this book. I spent many years as a teacher and senior leader believing that student voice was tokenistic. We would have a student council, which gave the impression of a school listening to its learners, but few points were actioned and many more empty promises were made for the future: 'We'll put it in our development plan next year.' I have sat in on governors' meetings where student representatives were given the first 30 minutes to report on student council meetings. The governors would listen intently, encourage and support, but then no action was taken. The students gain little from the process, but the school gains two big ticks in the 'impress the inspectors' book.

It is easy for a school to take a tokenistic approach, but I have gradually learned from my years in school leadership that it does more harm to an institution's ethos than schools might like to believe – for example, as a reason for a decline in behaviour. There are several advantages to genuinely investing time in listening to students:

● In an average school where students outnumber teachers ten to one, a sense of belonging will bring with it loyalty from the students towards the whole school community. They may not all feel they are being listened to consciously, but enough will appreciate that the school is attentive to their needs and concerns and recognises them as fully fledged members of the community with valid opinions. This will strengthen the collective desire to maintain a positive school ethos. I have worked in schools where this loyalty doesn't exist; those schools were failing on all counts.

● All schools aim to meet the educational, welfare and well-being needs of their students. Like any other successful organisation, it is imperative that we gain feedback from them if we are to improve our service – for example, through student representatives attending house/year meetings or student voice/council meetings. These encounters not only help to establish loyalty but also deepen the engagement of learners in the life of the school.

● Asking students for feedback on their learning in the classroom can lead to improvements in engagement and levels of achievement – for example:

  › Teachers questioning students in lessons to gauge their level of understanding and push for deeper thinking.

  › Mini whiteboards, traffic light systems (i.e. red, amber and green cards) and thumbs up, thumbs down or in the middle are all methods to evaluate understanding and adjust the learning accordingly.

  › Feedback from learners in their books, such as describing what went well or what they could have done to improve the work, enables the teacher to personalise future lessons, identify whole-class difficulties and plan future lessons.

These methods are used most often by teachers. However, just as effective (although in my experience used less frequently) are exit cards, which give students the opportunity to judge the teacher's performance. Not only do they give teachers valuable feedback concerning student understanding of the lesson (which will help with future planning), but they also help the teacher to reflect on their own performance. An example can be found in Cog 3.4.

Most schools have a student council (or use student voice) to help them better understand young people's needs and wants. This will have some influence on school policy and contribute towards creating a real sense of belonging. But is it enough? Giving young people control over what, how, where and when they learn will create an even greater feeling of connection with their school. This, in turn, will encourage students to engage with the school not only as a partner in their learning journey, but also as a resource to help them make sense of all the information they imbibe on a daily basis outside of school, deepening their understanding of the world.

This brings us back to blended learning and an acceptance that some learning can take place outside of school – at home or in other community spaces. This enables students to use the school more as a hub for learning, rather than as a building where traditional lessons take place. Are we ready to trust our students' abilities to take on more ownership of their learning? Student autonomy is a big hurdle to cross, but it isn't insurmountable for students of secondary school age. Unfortunately, although blended learning can increase the sense of belonging a young person has for his or her school, schools are reluctant to implement it, mainly due to the accountability constraints we face. Schools like to remain in control.

6. Recognise achievement and success

Young people need constant praise and recognition for their achievements and other successes. We all do this in schools to motivate and encourage our students. However, it is important to draw a distinction between praise or recognition and rewards. Praise and recognition should be used to draw out and highlight the intrinsic motivation for doing something, while rewards offer extrinsic motivation.

Extrinsic motivation might improve the behaviours you want to see, but these are often short term and the behaviours will disappear if the reward is taken away. Studies also show that they detract from the intrinsic reasons for participating and doing your best in an activity.[14] Rewards have always been a challenge for schools. Younger year groups love achievement points, but as children grow older they can come to seem a little childish. A 15-year-old is just not going to put in the extra effort to earn enough points for a pencil case from the reward shop.

This is where work ethic comes into the frame. Up until now, I have not explicitly touched on this aspect of ethos, which some may argue should be a central focus in schools. This has been deliberate as I believe that the four aspects of ethos we have explored in this book – insightful leadership; vision, purpose and direction; care and positive relationships; and belonging and inclusiveness – all contribute towards creating a strong work ethos. Having said that, the most explicit thing we can do to encourage our students (and staff) to be conscientious is to highlight the importance of intrinsic motivation.

When I was a vice principal, during the early days of academies in England, schools were given a grant to improve GCSE results. In our school, someone on the leadership team proposed that we give monetary rewards to students: the higher the grade, the more money they would be awarded. The rationale was that middle-class families already rewarded their children financially and so had an advantage over those from less affluent homes.

At the time, I argued vociferously against the suggestion. I instinctively felt it was wrong because it would undermine the reason for exams – the inherent reward from achieving good results. The proposal nevertheless went through in our academy and remained in place for a few years until it was gradually phased out. Ultimately, there was no evidence that it worked. Our results were already rising but this could not be attributed to the rewards. The money was given out after results day and so was too remote to provide much motivation while the students were still in school.

Over the years, I have witnessed many effective ways of recognising success:

- If a student does something well in class or around the school, don't miss the opportunity to praise them and acknowledge what has been done (e.g. thumbs up, smile, note in a book, public praise).

---

14 See, for example, Tod Rejholic, 'An Action Research on the Effects of Extrinsic Rewards on Motivation of Eighth Grade Language Arts Students' (2002). Available at: https://files.eric.ed.gov/fulltext/ED473051.pdf.

- Always remind students about the benefits of behaving in a certain way around the school (to make it a nicer environment for us all to work in) and the advantages of working hard.

- Frequent recognition assemblies to encourage an ethos of celebrating success. (In schools where aspirations are low this can be a battle at first, with the students reluctant to be recognised. However, the more it happens, the more it becomes accepted as the norm.)

- Postcards or calls home to applaud achievements.

- Regular meetings with the head (biscuits and drinks) in his or her office to recognise success. (It is also a good opportunity to gather some feedback from students.)

- Privilege areas in the school for those who are motivated or working beyond expectations and achieving.

These are all forms of recognition that are motivating but don't detract from the intrinsic motivation to work hard. There are forms of extrinsic motivation too but they need to be used with caution:

- Achievement points that go towards gifts, tokens and so on. They work well with younger children but tend to fizzle out in older year groups. The reward that goes with them isn't necessarily the most potent motivator; the actual achievement point is recognition enough for most students.

- Reward trips or prizes at the end of term. This is a nice way to recognise success but it does not necessarily motivate students during the year as the reward is too distant.

The best motivator I have found for boosting a sense of belonging is to send a birthday card to every child in the school each year. The admin staff would address the envelopes and, on a Friday, give me a pile of those who were due birthdays in the following week. This was a huge hit with the students, who always used to thank me for the card. It definitely created a connection for them with the school.

To sum up: the relentless recognition of hard work, commitment and achievement will create a deeper sense of belonging than more abstract rewards. Bringing people together to celebrate can also create a strong feeling of community and can be more powerful than rewards given to an individual.

Cog 4.3: The blocks to creating a sense of belonging for young people

No matter what you are trying to introduce or develop, there are always obstacles. It goes with the territory of school leadership. But they need not become immovable obstructions. Compromise may be required at times, but most difficulties can be overcome.

Let us consider the initiatives discussed in the previous cog – what blocks might we face, and how might we overcome them?

Costs

Sadly, money always seems to be the first hurdle. If you are a head, you will no doubt have been tallying up the costs of creating a sense of belonging in your school as you have been reading this chapter. The section on support staff in Cog 4.2 alone is probably enough to make your finance officer bolt their office door and hire an armed guard to stand outside it. But is it really so costly?

Skim through that cog again with a financial hat on and consider the actual cost of additional support staff. I have always regarded it as an investment. I am in my third headship, and in each of my schools I have prioritised spending on pastoral staff: full-time non-teaching year/house heads, learning mentors, child protection officers and counsellors. Much of the financing has come from student deprivation grants, but it has also required some painful restructuring processes in order to make savings elsewhere in the school. (It is amazing how many schools have long-standing roles that have never been questioned or rationalised.) This may sound harsh, but the reality is that schools provide a service which should be organised and implemented to serve the best interests of our students. If this requires a reorganisation of staffing, then we shouldn't shy away from it.

We will examine community involvement in Cog 4.5. This might entail, at a minimum, a teaching and learning responsibility payment for the teacher willing to take on the role of coordinator. This might begin to scratch the surface, but unless you also reduce their teaching load significantly, then maintaining meaningful contacts would be unsustainable. For this reason, I have argued for a community officer appointment instead. If you get the job description right and a good person in post, your school can be transformed. Posts can then be created which can in theory pay for themselves, providing the school site is being used to its full potential for community use.

As life expectancy continues to increase, the potential for volunteers as a resource will surely grow. This presents some possible opportunities for reducing costs – for example:

- Sugata Mitra set up his Granny Cloud in 2009 using retired teachers in India to help teach English to Indian schoolchildren. This has since been expanded into a worldwide network.[15]

- Although Eastern High is not a church school, we have developed strong ties with a local church group who provide mentoring, youth worker support and extracurricular assistance in a wide range of activities.

- Many universities offer student mentors and career workshops for young people.

- Local charities can offer support. During the COVID-19 pandemic school closures, charities helped us to fund many projects, including setting up a food bank and assisting us to collect and provide reading books to all students.

All of these examples will improve the welfare and well-being of young people, and so will reduce the demand for additional services in schools and thereby the need to develop as many support roles.

---

15 See Carole Cadwalladr, 'The Granny Cloud: The Network of Volunteers Helping Poorer Children Learn', *The Guardian* (2 August 2015). Available at: https://www.theguardian.com/education/2015/aug/02/sugata-mitra-school-in-the-cloud. See also http://thegrannycloud.org.

Time and energy

If I am being honest, every time someone comes to me with a new initiative and I decide not to go ahead with it, I always use cost as my go-to excuse – in particular, the cost of the initial set-up in terms of time. Time costs money, especially when you calculate the cover implications required to establish a new scheme. There are also the knock-on effects of the disruption to student learning.

This is where head teachers have to be forward-thinking, strategic and ask questions such as:

- Is this a priority for the school?
- Will the outcomes justify the time and money invested?
- Will the outcomes justify the initial disruption?
- Do we (as individuals and as a whole school) have the energy to see this through?

The final point is probably the biggest subliminal block, so we must be realistic about our expectations and capacity. A good leader must be aware of the breaking point for staff and not tip a school into crisis because they do not have the time or energy to do things properly.

Cog 4.4: Creating a sense of belonging for staff

We all know how stressful and overwhelming teaching – and, for that matter, any role in a school – can be at times. For this reason, it goes without saying that all school staff need to be looked after, to feel valued and nurtured and, above all, to quickly develop a sense of belonging to their school community. Staff who are cared for in this way will contribute to the continuous growth and development of their school.

What follows are some examples that have helped me to create a sense of belonging among staff.

Vision

Early on in my first headship, a new member of staff approached me in the corridor and asked if he could have a few moments of my time. He then went on to ask me about the vision and direction of the school. My first thought was: didn't you read up on this when you were applying for the job? I kept my opinions to myself, though, and instead led him back to my office where we discussed the vision fully. At the end he thanked me and said, 'I needed to know that because I didn't think I could become really involved in the school unless I was clear about what you and the school were trying to achieve.'

This teacher wanted to make an impression not only in the classroom but also across the whole school. He was turning up for work, teaching lessons, having some social interaction with staff, going home and marking. However, he didn't feel that he was a part of something. He had real insight to ask me about the school vision, and subsequently went on to become a valued member of staff.

This episode made me realise that although the question raised by this teacher was a rarity, it was likely that there were many others feeling the same way (possibly unconsciously). It made me go back and look at what we had written on our website and prospectus from a different standpoint. There was a clear vision statement, but it wasn't connected to the life of the school on a day-to-day basis. Instead it stood alone as a set of grandiose assertions and didn't connect with what the school was doing.

Since then, I have always made sure to share the school vision with staff through a chart that explores how it connects with the various aspects of the school, and, in the case of my current school, the four purposes of the new curriculum for Wales (see the example on page 183).

With this in place, displayed prominently and discussed regularly, it isn't long until staff feel fully involved and part of a purposeful organisation moving forward.

Professional development

Professional development is an obvious consideration and doesn't need much elaboration in terms of developing practice. If it is related to school priorities, professional development is an investment in time and money for the SLT and helps to focus the member of staff on the school's vision and priorities. Professional development that is more relevant to the individual requires you, as a leader, to determine the balance between giving a member of staff time off to study an area that is possibly not of benefit to the school against them feeling supported and valued.

This is often not an easy one to solve. I have found it useful to create a spreadsheet listing the courses and other professional development courses that members of staff have attended, which helps to ensure that all staff have equal opportunities for development and justifies any requests that are turned down.

Don't forget the negative impact that staff absence can have on a school too. It is vital, therefore, that there are clear procedures for requesting leave for professional development reasons. Each request needs to be made in good time, so there is sufficient time to consider it against other staff absences or events happening in school on the same day.

	The learning habits we will develop	Our pledge to learners	Our expectations of learners	Our improvement priorities
Sustainable, effective and meaningful approaches to learning				
Sustainable relationships and partnerships				
Sustainable mind, body and soul				
Sustainable use of resources and the environment				

Capability versus support

I first became aware of capability procedures when I first joined a leadership team. Initially, I was shocked that this sort of thing happened (this was the mid-nineties and accountability in schools was just taking off). Like all schools, the head dreaded a poor Ofsted report and so had commenced capability procedures on a number of staff. (This was taken to new levels when academies first opened and the pressure was on from central government to ensure they were a success. Their 'silent assassins' would regularly turn up to pass judgement on people, beginning with the SLT.)

Since then, the constant pressure to ensure that all teachers are working at their full capacity, all of the time, has gradually hardened me to the need to take staff through the capability procedures process. There have been some fantastically successful turnarounds, as well as others who have had to leave the school or the profession. Some may agree to differ, but I like to think that those individuals who left weren't right for teaching. Of those who did leave, the majority found employment they are better suited to and are happier for it.

My views began to change following a visit to a school some years ago which claimed to have no capability procedures process. In fact, it turned out that they removed staff in other less transparent ways. However, it made me wonder whether it was possible to develop staff to a level where capability need never be an option. Surely, if staff were to have a true sense of belonging in the school community, then we had to support them as far as possible when things weren't going well in the classroom.

When I began my second headship, the staff were on tenterhooks. It felt as if they were constantly looking over their shoulder and waiting for me to pounce. It is hard enough trying to gain the trust of a new staff body, but when you have come from a school where there was a high turnover of staff, largely due to capability, your reputation is going to precede you.

I wanted to say to them, 'Look, I'm not like that. Honest! I just want the best for our students, so if we all try our best there's nothing to worry about.' I knew it was pointless. I wasn't going to become an idealist and assume that everyone would do their best and improve with support. Sadly, there are some individuals who hide their insecurities by becoming a negative influence or energy drain. In every school, I have come across people who seem to give the impression that they don't want the school to succeed – possibly because they don't believe they can measure up to the level expected of them if the whole school is successful.

To help me clarify my own thoughts regarding the ability and willingness of teaching staff, I have developed the performance matrix below. I have a slide for each term and year and I move the names around to monitor an individual's progress.

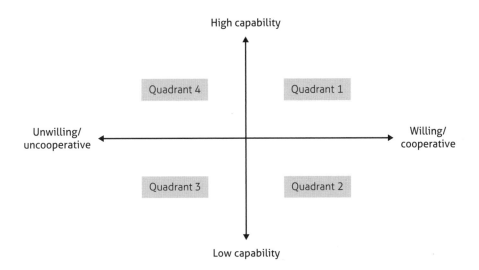

- In quadrant 1, I would place the teachers who are on board, willing and very good teachers. I would look to these staff to coach and support others.

- In quadrant 2, I would place the teachers who were on board and willing but not such competent teachers – for example, early career teachers or members of staff who have previously lacked support. I would promise myself that I would support them as much as possible.

- In quadrant 3, I would place the teachers who were not on board, negative influences and uncooperative. It is likely that they are also poor teachers. It would be my priority to move these teachers into quadrant 2 or 4 in the first instance, before hopefully moving them on to quadrant 1. However, if there was no response then I would take more formal action.

- In quadrant 4, I would place those who were good teachers but not on board and negative influences in the school. These teachers would be destined for a one-to-one discussion with me.

It is essential to put in place some kind of systematic approach for all aspects of improvement, staff included. I have found this matrix to be a very useful tool for thinking strategically about staff development when faced with a school that is failing its children. It is for my personal use only (I don't share it with staff – at the most a deputy) and it is definitely not an exact science, but it has helped me reduce to almost zero the need for capability procedures.

Very much like the road map discussed in Cog 1.4, recreating the performance matrix every term and adjusting the position of teachers' names has enabled me to show progress as we work with staff systematically. Inspectors like the fact that we know our staff and it gives the message that we are being proactive about school improvement.

Obviously, the aim is not to have anyone in quadrant 3. This has to involve frank (and at times difficult) conversations about the person's willingness to follow the guidance and coaching that is on offer. It is also about whether or not the person is happy in the school or in their chosen career. For example, offering staff external mental health or well-being support has been a great success. In my current school, we initially employed a psychotherapist to come in each week and offer confidential sessions for staff. It helped many individuals to work through issues and difficulties they had with the school or their job. Sometimes this involved exploring personal matters from outside school that were affecting their performance or attitude in school.

As result, many members of staff moved into quadrant 2 where we could focus on developing their teaching practice and pedagogy. However, it doesn't work for everyone. At some point, those who won't budge out of quadrant 3 have to be addressed if the school is to continue providing the very best it can for its students.

The big success comes with moving teachers from quadrant 2 to quadrant 1. Putting aside the early career teachers, these are staff who may have been floundering for years without ever being offered the proper support. Given time, energy and a personalised programme of support (often using those teachers from quadrant 1), these individuals begin to see the practical benefits of support in terms of less stress, improved relationships with students and, in many cases, reduced workload.

Teacher voice

Quite early on in my career I worked in a school in London where staff morale had fallen to an all-time low following its first Ofsted inspection (one of the first in the country), which was a spectacular failure. There was a lot of camaraderie in the staffroom and people supported each other through many difficult experiences. However, following numerous serious incidents – including some students burning down a wing of the school – the staff had begun to complain in the staffroom, myself included. The trouble was that we had a new head who didn't know about our concerns or needs, and apart from involving the unions (which at the time didn't have a good relationship with the school) we felt we had no voice.

In the end, we nominated a representative who would meet with the head regularly and discuss concerns affecting staff. Names were never mentioned and the individual was seen as a voice for the whole staff body. It resulted in the workforce feeling listened to, especially when they saw action taking place.

One of the hardest aspects of being a head is not receiving feedback from staff. If you ask someone to their face how things are, you will seldom get the answer they want to give – sometimes not even from members of your senior team. Is that because everyone is fearful of me personally? I would like to think not; I think it is more to do with the role itself. I am constantly begging staff to tell me when they have concerns, but no matter how hard I try, there are always some who prefer not to voice their doubts.

I try to encourage members of staff to form a staff association with a chair who meets with me regularly. This separates union-type issues from more general well-being issues. Where this has happened, the staff have felt listened to and I have learned a great deal. I also tend to carry out anonymous surveys, which I have learned to use sparingly as staff soon become bored of them and don't respond. I have even gone as far as to put suggestion boxes in the staff toilets and staffroom in an attempt to gauge people's feelings. In short, as I say to staff regularly: I can't improve the school for you if I don't know what you want.

Another way to gather opinions has been to meet individually with every member of staff. A 20–30 minute meeting once a year is a real investment in time. I haven't always managed it, but when I do, I never regret it. It helps people to feel they are being listened to and recognised. I keep notes of their needs and wants and try to categorise them into broad areas to be addressed.

Social events and recognition

Staff feel they belong when they can socialise and take part in activities together. I used to look at corporate team-building exercises disparagingly, until I was persuaded by my senior team to allow them to organise one for our staff body. At that time, I was still fairly new to the school and although it was beginning to improve, staff were still on a high state of alert. The day we organised was run by an external organisation and involved physical and mental team challenges. It was a great success which bonded staff and was spoken about for years afterwards.

So, why haven't I run one again? The simple answer is: I should have done. As heads, we can become very complacent about staff morale. We can be working hand to address their needs and imagining we are doing a good job, but it isn't until we introduce something different, such as a team-building day, that previously unconscious needs come to the fore. If they can be addressed, this creates an even deeper sense of belonging.

Staff social nights out are also essential in creating a feeling of connection. I have not been good at attending these as a head, mainly because I inevitably end up pinned against the bar being asked awkward work-related questions by an 'over happy' member of staff. However, I have learned that people really do appreciate the attendance of the head and senior team. I wouldn't recommend staying all night, but spending enough time to talk to most people is well worthwhile, with the added bonus of giving you that feeling of camaraderie you can so easily lose when you become a head.

Personal recognition is probably one of the most important contributing factors to a member of staff developing a sense of belonging. Often, I look at all of the extra things that some staff are doing altruistically and I wish I could reward them in some way. I wish there could be some form of recognised financial reward system in place – I would pay some people double if I could – but there isn't. I have tried many ways of recognising individual efforts and successes, but it can be like walking a tightrope.

Boxes of chocolates in offices at Christmas time, Creme Eggs in pigeonholes at Easter and cakes every so often have never met with any complaints, although unfortunately there are always some who will say I am trying to buy favour (no need to say what quadrant these staff fall into!). These kinds of remarks will shake you to the core; however, I know that the vast majority appreciate that we are trying to acknowledge all the extras that staff do in the best and fairest way we can.

Staff turnover

The ethos underlying a school should be stronger than any individual and be able to withstand the changes in staffing a school faces on a year-by-year basis. If we consider the other aspects of ethos mentioned in this book so far, they all contribute to the development of a sense of belonging as well as forming the foundations of a school ethos. The length of time a member of staff has served in a school should not affect the overall ethos, if the school follows the principles we have considered so far.

There are advantages and disadvantages for individuals and for schools with respect to length of service. Personally, I have always felt that six years in one school has been about right for me. It gives me enough time to settle in, develop my practice and instigate initiatives that have time to embed. I also feel that when you focus on one thing (or, as a head teacher, one school), then you sometimes need someone with a fresh pair of eyes and new energy to take over. The lesson here for schools is that people do move on, so it is essential that no one works in isolation on important projects. Succession planning is vital in ensuring that projects or initiatives can carry on seamlessly when a leader or manager leaves.

While it is healthy to have a fairly regular turnover of staff, who will bring in fresh ideas and new energy (providing the ethos in the school is strong and established), there are also advantages to having well-established, long-serving staff members. These individuals are often held in high regard by the local community and bring invaluable local knowledge to the school. Parents who attended the same school as their child often feel comforted when they see a familiar face. Even if they perceived that teacher as having terrorised them during their school days, nostalgia frequently overrides any grievances they once held. Parents also recognise the loyalty that the teacher may be showing to the school and value them for that.

High levels of staff turnover will be felt especially acutely by vulnerable students who crave for stability in their lives, but a rapidly changing staff body will undoubtedly make it more difficult to create a sense of belonging among all students. In addition, a high staff renewal rate may also create issues in relation to recruitment (especially in rural areas) and a lack of continuity.

To summarise, whether a member of staff is long-standing or has only been at the school for a year, they can all share equally in a sense of belonging with the school community. Ensuring that all staff understand the vision of the school and know they are supported, both in terms of their own professional development and practice and their mental health and well-being, is time and money well spent.

Cog 4.5: The importance of the school in its community

As a head, I have always started each year full of good intentions. However, when it comes to partnership working, 'stuff' often takes over as the year progresses, especially in schools with challenging circumstances. We might set up a parent forum and then become disheartened when the first few sessions have a low turn-out. We might establish a link with a local business and develop activities with them in school, such as mentoring, work experience or curriculum projects, but the partnership all too often fizzles out.

There is no excuse for not getting involved with the local community: the investment can be a win-win for all concerned. As a deputy head, I worked in a school that employed a small community team which developed a range of solid partnerships with other organisations and individuals in the local areas. It organised a wide range of community-linked activities for the school, such as curriculum projects, weekend and holiday activities (for students and adults), evening classes for parents, and sport events; we even held weddings in the school.

The better the links are between secondary and primary schools, the more parents of primary-aged children are likely to have confidence in the school, and consequently have fewer worries about sending their child to the school. In addition, the earlier children in feeder primary schools know that the local secondary school 'belongs' to them, the better. Regular organised visits for arts or sporting events, science, technology or languages lessons are all worth the effort to organise. Collaborative working in partnership with feeder primary schools regarding curriculum development and delivery is an essential way to ensure that learning is consistently relevant throughout a young person's education.

These may seem obvious points, but we shouldn't underestimate the importance of making local connections. I have worked in and visited some amazing community-focused schools and seen the impact first hand. The more people get to know the school, the more their belief with the school vision grows, and the more likely they are to invest their energy and resources into it.

Creating a sense of belonging among the community

We have explored the importance that community involvement has in developing a school ethos in young people, who feel they have some ownership of the school. But the school, in turn, also needs to have a sense of belonging within the community it serves. The school should be responsible for creating this connection, if it is to build confidence in its ability to serve all of the community and especially its young residents.

There are local agendas in all communities, so it is essential as a head, particularly if you are new to the area, that you do your homework on those individuals who have concerns about your school, however innocuous they may seem. I have twice faced the problem of a community that has lost confidence in its local school and is consequently on the lookout for problems. Under these circumstances, the journey towards easing this tension and regaining support can be long and fraught with difficulty.

For example, the local community of Bristol Brunel Academy had experienced several running battles in the streets immediately outside the school, all race related. An exclusion zone had been created by the police to prevent groups of more than three young people from congregating. As a consequence, people assumed that any fight between students that occurred on the premises or in the surrounding area straight after school was race related, even before the incident had been investigated. As a result, the academy was in danger of being labelled, like its predecessor, as a school that didn't do enough for its black and minority ethnic (BAME) community. We had to work hard during the first few years to dispel this belief. We worked especially closely with the Somali community and employed several Somali youth workers. Within three years, we had moved from being an academy with 90% white British students to a population with 40% BAME students, which reflected the local demographic. However, it took longer than this to overcome the underlying fear of further race-based incidents.

In your first year (or if the community is in a high state of alert, in your first term), one of your key priorities is to be well informed about the rumours doing the rounds in the locality. Without the support and trust of the community, you will be in demand constantly by concerned parents and other stakeholders. All your time needs to be focused on developing and improving your school, but facing 300-plus emails each evening isn't very conducive to either a healthy work–life balance or focusing on your core purpose.

Although it is tiring, you will be full of momentum when you first take up a new headship. Invest this energy to free up time for yourself later on by doing some or all of the following to reassure your community in the first few months about the ethos you are creating.

Parents

- Write to parents. Introduce yourself and describe your vision and plans. Assure them that you are tackling any specific or commonly known issues.

- Hold information evenings to elaborate on what you have said in your letter but also to field any questions. It is worth taking questions on the night from the audience rather than individually later on, as it shows you are happy to communicate and discuss things openly. It also gives people the opportunity to listen to how well you deal with queries and will instil a sense of calm and ease when they see how confident you are.

- Hold meetings in local community centres if the turnout is low at school. Some parents don't like going into schools and feel more confident in environments they know well. Later on, you can work at getting them into school.

- Meet with anyone who comes in demanding to see the head initially. Once they know you, you will be able to pass on these requests to other appropriate members of staff.

- Make sure everyone knows how you will communicate with them. Keep your social networks up to date: the school website, Twitter, Facebook or whatever social media platform is in vogue at the time.

Local primaries/clusters

- Go to cluster meetings if they occur. A deputy may take over this duty in time but you must also go at first. Not only do primary heads need to get to know you as soon as possible, but they also need to get to know other local heads. It is all about reassuring people that you know about local issues and are there to help alleviate them by working in partnership.

- Use local primaries to communicate with prospective parents by letting them know your school news. You can do this via letters or regular updates for their noticeboard or newsletters.

- Have a stand at Year 5 and 6 parents' evenings; it is important that you are there to talk about your school.

Community groups

- Find out what the main influential community or neighbourhood groups are and contact them – for example, religious groups, business consortiums (e.g. Rotary Club) and neighbourhood-based organisations. Ask if you can attend a meeting to introduce yourself and tell them about your vision for the school.

The primary aim is not to involve all these bodies in new school initiatives; quite the opposite. What you must do first is to find out what they know about the school and apprise them of your vision and priorities. The former will help you to find out more about community impressions of your school and the latter will (hopefully) help to develop their confidence in you and in the future capacity of the school to improve. By all means tell them that you would like to work with them, and fully intend to do so, but you will do so gradually and only when you have fully assessed the current state of the school. This will assure them that you will be able to commit to any future partnership fully.

Local politicians, local authority key figures and governors

- Invite them in to look around. If the school is in crisis they might notice things you would rather they didn't see, but it is better to be transparent. Explain with conviction how you intend to deal with any issues that emerge. Let them know how hard the job will be (if this is the case); you may find additional resources coming your way. (This happened at Eastern High where I gained extra funding to make repairs to our old buildings and for additional youth worker support.)

- Listen to them, find out their concerns and take note of them. As with any of the groups mentioned above, they should form part of any self-evaluation and future improvement plans.

- Ask them to spread the word that the school is being led and managed effectively and that it will improve. Ensure they understand that this will take time; they must be patient. Let them know that you will keep them informed about any developments. Responding to their emails and writing a regular community newsletter (sent out by your PA) will likely keep them happy and interested.

Unions

- Unions are just as much a part of your community as the other groups and individuals listed above. If you are starting in a school that you know will require a restructure or where you are likely to instigate capability procedures, then it is essential to meet your local trade union representatives as soon as possible. Acknowledge the school union representatives and listen to their concerns, but ensure that you organise a meeting with the local or regional union representatives. (When I first arrived at Eastern High, the local authority suggested I should do this due to the level of crisis the school was facing. It was the best piece of advice I received. I wish I had done it in previous schools.)

- When meeting with union representatives, it is important to emphasise that you want to engage with them as professional bodies who not only look after the interests of their members but who also uphold the standards and values of the profession. It is vital they understand that you have the same goals as they do with respect to this. Be transparent regarding the likelihood of capability procedures for some staff (if this is the case). Tell them that you will keep them abreast of all developments and look forward to their help and support in creating an outstanding environment and ethos for their members.

I have been lucky with the union representatives with whom I have worked. I know some heads who have almost resigned in frustration due to the constant back-and-forth negotiations with teacher unions. The key is to keep them informed and involve them fully in the process.

Cog 4.6: Personalisation and inclusiveness

When it comes to creating a sense of belonging, personalisation and inclusiveness are the most obvious elements. Most people would agree that schools should strive to maximise the chances for their students by personalising the curriculum offer and ensuring they are included equally in all aspects of school life. Get it right and no student will feel disenfranchised. But it is not easy.

Differentiation or personalisation?

Differentiation and personalisation are often used interchangeably in schools. I prefer to use the term personalisation when discussing a whole-school strategy; I see differentiation as a subsection of personalisation, based in classroom practice and focusing specifically on the different levels at which teachers set work and provide scaffolding. For the purposes of this cog, therefore, differentiation is the domain of teachers and teaching assistants in the classroom, while the greater (but not exclusive, as we will see below) responsibility for personalisation lies with school leaders.

If we are to provide both content that is meaningful to children (which will encourage them to come to school each day) and deliver a curriculum that is effective in preparing young people for life, then in addition to making it relevant, we must ensure that all students are appropriately challenged and engaged. Effective personalisation of the curriculum offer across the school and differentiated resources/ activities in the classroom enables students to see themselves as individuals and creates a feeling of belonging.

Differentiation in the classroom

As a teacher, I always struggled to differentiate work for students well. Even in classrooms which were set or banded with children of similar ability, I always felt I was letting down some individuals. We will return to the nuances of setting below, but for now we will focus on the practicalities of differentiation from the perspective of a school leader.

I have taught in schools, especially as an early career teacher, where the expectation was that we would create differentiated resources for every lesson, providing separate work for the less able, so they could work on the same topic alongside their peers, as well as extension work for the more able. It is easy for leaders to delegate this work to teachers and relatively straightforward to monitor the extent to which differentiation is taking place. However, the expectation that teachers should produce differentiated work in every lesson is an example of inflexible management and poor leadership. It does not consider the practicalities of doing this effectively: will the teacher have the time or the creativity to produce all of these different resources? And, if the work is rushed, how well will it meet the needs of the students?

As a leader responsible for monitoring the quality of teaching and learning, I don't look for differentiation in the classic sense of the term I have described above

– that is, resources and scaffolding. Instead, I am looking at the way learning is being managed in the classroom. For example:

- Are all the students making appropriate progress in each of the activities and tasks they carry out? If not, what is impeding their progress? Are there aspects of the lesson they can't access in terms of understanding or ability?

- Are all of the students suitably challenged (not too much to inhibit progress and not too little that the work is easy)?

- Has the differentiated work become a crutch for any students, making them overly dependent on the teacher? This also links to challenge: is the teacher encouraging resilience?

- Are differentiated resources given to students in a sensitive way? Some (more or less able students) may feel embarrassed to be treated differently from the majority of the class.

- How effective is the teaching assistant? Are they being managed efficiently by the teacher, perhaps supporting small groups with similar needs? If they are supporting one person, are they fostering resilience?

- Are the more able encouraged to go further and extend their understanding and skills?

- Is the teacher applying the 5M's (see Chapter 3) in a personalised way to ensure full participation?

- How well is the teacher using assessment for learning in the classroom, and when marking work to ensure the students know what they need to do to improve further? (This should take into account their ability range.)

- Has assessment informed planning?

As a school leader, I think it is worth spending time going through these points with staff. I still encounter teachers who feel guilty about not producing masses of resources that are individualised to the specific needs of their students. Differentiation is not just about discrete resources but rather the pedagogy that teachers adopt – that is, the methods used to enable young people to learn effectively. Planning to meet the needs of all students in the class need not be a time-consuming chore involving teachers spending countless hours producing resources. Effective differentiation and personalisation takes place in the learning interactions between teacher and students.

Whole-school personalisation and leadership

Whole-school personalisation is where we can begin to consider and implement a range of wide-scale interventions, such as the Reading Recovery literacy programme or extension and enrichment sessions for the more able. Most secondary schools already personalise their offer by reducing the curriculum at Key Stage 4 and allowing students to choose optional subjects in addition to the core subjects. This begins to separate some students from others, and in this manner, personalisation can come into conflict with the concept of a liberal education, which advocates broad learning for its own sake.

When we begin to set classes in specific subjects, we personalise to an even greater extent. However, in doing so we run the risk of narrowing the range of experiences that lower-attaining students have compared to their higher-attaining peers. The former may have fewer opportunities to partake in high-quality discussion, but the latter may also be disadvantaged by missing out on the chance to learn to work alongside, communicate with and understand those with needs that differ from their own. For example, they lose out on opportunities to develop compassion, patience and clear communication skills. These are the disadvantages that school leaders must balance against the advantages of a more personalised approach, targeted to meet the needs of a specific group of students.

Streaming whole year groups, so that every child in every class is with students of a similar ability, is an even more extreme form of personalisation, although it seldom happens in schools in the UK today. The tripartite system, which existed from the post-war years until the mid-seventies, and still exists in a few local authorities, goes even further by separating students of different abilities into different schools (grammar, secondary technical and secondary modern).

The recommendations of the Warnock Report resulted in the 1981 Education Act and a more inclusive view of educating those with additional learning needs.[16] The report paved the way to schools developing differentiated work and introducing setting rather than streaming. Its liberal values – which strongly advocated for everyone's right to have access to a broad and balanced curriculum – have been long-lived and are still relevant in our schools today.

....

16 Mary Warnock, *Report of the Committee of Enquiry into the Education of Handicapped Children and Young People* [Warnock Report] (London: HMSO, 1978). A useful summary can be found at: http://www. educationengland.org.uk/documents/warnock where there is also a link to the full report.

Although I have always supported the values enshrined in the Warnock Report, in more recent years I have hit on a problem because I would like to implement initiatives in my school that I believe are right but possibly challenge some of these values. The more schools are hit by cuts and the loss of the government-sponsored and charitable support services that were once available, the more I am having to come to terms with a more pragmatic side to my educational aspirations.

What we are doing in respect of personalisation currently, especially in schools in deprived areas, is unsatisfactory. The system is failing far too many, with over one in ten young people aged between 16 and 24 not in education or employment.[17] We are disenfranchising many of our students by having unrealistic expectations for them and by throwing them into an accountability system that is not designed for them.

I walk into classes on a daily basis and watch certain students struggle with certain subjects they simply should not be studying. Either they can't see the relevance of it to their own lives or the work is too difficult at a conceptual level; as a result, they are destined at best to gain a low mark or at worst to fail altogether. There are many reasons for this: poor levels of numeracy and literacy, not enough support at home, adverse childhood experiences, inadequate attachment to others, unhelpful beliefs and values, and a lack of motivation caused by any of the above and more.

I am also pressurised by the parents of more able children who want them to be in fast-track classes and not held back by their peers. Of course, this shouldn't be necessary if the teaching and learning in the classroom addresses the points listed in the previous section, but if I am being realistic, I know that sometimes it can be required.

It is a dilemma. On the one hand, I believe it is right for young people from a range of backgrounds, cultures and abilities to learn together in school because it prepares them for the real world. On the other hand, it isn't reasonable for them all to study the same subjects and the same number of subjects because that isn't supportive of the needs of the individual. However, by segregating and offering different subjects or methodologies (e.g. vocational rather than academic

---

17 Office for National Statistics, 'Young People Not in Education, Employment or Training (NEET), UK: August 2020'. Available at: https://www.ons.gov.uk/employmentandlabourmarket/peoplenotinwork/ unemployment/bulletins/youngpeoplenotineducationemploymentortrainingneet/august2020.

education) for some students, we may be preventing them from accessing the richness of the full curriculum and all that life and culture have to offer.

It is unfortunate that schools in deprived areas continually have to play catch-up to close the attainment gap between students from lower- and higher-income families. The Education Endowment Foundation have carried out extensive analysis into how effective schools have been in closing this gap and noted an improvement for young people from disadvantaged backgrounds.[18] However, they also accept that the rate of improvement is slow and will take decades for the disparity to close. In short, the interventions we are putting in place have some impact but not enough, and more intervention doesn't necessarily help students over the longer term.

This raises the following question: are we distracted from providing an education that is capable of meeting the needs of all young people by the real elephant in the room – namely, how we recognise and measure attainment and progress at the age of 16? In the UK, we routinely think of individual attainment and school performance in terms of how well our students perform at 16. We do this automatically; it is hardwired into us and we don't question it. GCSEs are a very efficient and relatively simple way to compare students and schools, but as a species we are certainly not simple. We develop at different rates, we have different starts in life and we have different cultural backgrounds, all of which combine to create a variety of needs, tastes and interests. Should we be measuring the success of *all* students in exactly the same way?

While many schools in deprived areas struggle to find ways to enable over 50% of each cohort to attain the Level 2 benchmark, I believe that we could guarantee almost all of our school-leavers meaningful progression routes, at the correct level and with guaranteed employment opportunities (regardless of whether or not they decide not to follow an academic path). However, if we choose to lead our less academically minded students down alternative, non-academic routes, this personalised strategy would challenge the values enshrined in the Warnock Report.

I have considered various ways of personalising the curriculum offer in a sensitive way for the most able and the least able, such as a 'school within a school' model. This approach does involve streaming. For example, a secondary school might

---

18 Education Endowment Foundation, *The Attainment Gap 2017* (2018). Available at: https://educationendowmentfoundation.org.uk/public/files/Annual_Reports/EEF_Attainment_Gap_Report_2018.pdf.

choose to employ some primary teachers to deliver a transitional nurture curriculum for a small number of learners in Years 7 and 8 (possibly more if the need is there). This could be justified if it is clear that the students would not fare well in a mainstream setting. Ideally, this would be based on a revolving door model, with reviews taking place each half-term and the students moving into the mainstream or out of the mainstream into one of the nurture groups as required.

In schools that adopt a three-year Key Stage 4, for those students from Year 9 onwards who are still unable to access the full curriculum, a similar programme could be implemented that has English and maths at its core but also various life skill qualifications and apprenticeships, in partnership with a local further education college. These apprenticeships could be multi-skilled initially, but begin to focus more on a particular trade as the learners progress through the programme.

Another alternative is to create a more able and talented school within the school, where eligible students follow an extended curriculum which challenges them at an appropriate level. The main argument for this approach is that the less able will not feel so stigmatised by being assigned to a 'bottom' set.

There is no easy answer. However, schools that adopt a personalised model must ensure that groups are formed on the basis of rigorous analysis of student information. There must also be clear exit opportunities back into mainstream, where appropriate. At Key Stage 4, students will have to remain committed to their course, although tasters in Year 9, accompanied by good careers advice, should help to reduce the number of dropouts. In this way, personalised learning at a whole-school level can result in greater opportunities for all.

In effect, I have described a school that has had to reinvent itself. At the time of writing, schools no longer have the external supporting structures they once had, and I don't believe it will return in the near future. If we are to ensure that all our students maintain a sense of belonging and no one becomes disenfranchised, we must look at new and alternative strategies. This may challenge our values and necessitate some prioritisation when it comes to meeting the needs of the child – for example, do we put a broad education before the ability to access that education? (Which is a good reason to read Chapter 2 again!) Do you have a rationale for your actions, and are they based on sound principles?

Cog 4.7: Embracing diversity

We have only scratched the surface of the issues around personalisation in the previous cog and, unfortunately, this will also apply when we consider diversity and equality in schools. However, a school ethos will never be comprehensive if it does not take into account the voice and needs of every student and member of staff.

Embracing diversity fully in schools falls into four categories:

1   Having an awareness of the strengths, needs and concerns of particular groups, as well as the possible inequalities or threats they may face (i.e. disability, race, ethnicity, gender, religion and sexuality).

2   Being pre-emptive in identifying any instances where any of these groups may come up against prejudice, inequality or exclusion.

3   Having the ability to support the concerns of these groups and manage issues sensitively and appropriately.

4   Being proactive in celebrating diversity and the richness it can bring to a school.

Hidden prejudice and unconscious bias

It is so easy for a head to walk around a school and think, yes, we are all one happy family here. We can become complacent very quickly if students or staff aren't communicating their concerns. We can also readily forget that for some groups, prejudice and inequality is so commonplace that it is expected and almost the norm, and so incidents are often not reported.

In one school where I worked, we had a reporting system which measured a student's approach to learning by giving them scores against certain domains – in this instance, Guy Claxton's 4R's (resilience, resourcefulness, reflectiveness and reciprocity). We gave each student a score out of five for each R. We were able to use the information to check which students were improving on which measure and which students were declining (we carried out the report five times a year). We could also find out which teachers might not be giving accurate scores and which teachers had possible issues with certain students.

We then began to delve more deeply and looked at the scores of black Afro-Caribbean students against white British students. We found that white teachers gave scores to black students which were on average lower than those they gave to white students. We also found that our black Afro-Caribbean teachers gave scores to black students which were in line with or higher than the scores they gave to white students. We couldn't believe what we were seeing, but a few rounds of reports showed this to be a consistent trend. It raised a number of questions for us:

- Were our white teachers prejudiced against black Afro-Caribbean students, perhaps due to long-term institutional racism or preconceived perceptions?

- Were our black Afro-Caribbean teachers prejudiced in favour of black Afro-Caribbean students?

- Were our black Afro-Caribbean teachers more understanding or tolerant of black Afro-Caribbean students because they came from the same cultural background and therefore could recognise positive traits that perhaps white teachers couldn't?

This exercise resulted in us listening more to teacher and student voice, opening up frank discussions and looking for collective solutions. To ensure that this awareness didn't fade away, we made sure that the scrutiny and discussion of scores became commonplace. (We also wanted to check that scores didn't drift in the other direction but remain as a fair reflection of student progress.)

This was a lesson for me early on and has ensured that I don't become complacent. However, it hasn't meant that I do it well. My teenage daughter reinforced this one day when she said: 'Dad, what do you know? You're middle-aged, white, straight and male.' It's true. How can I have genuine empathy with people from another race, class, gender or sexuality? Reni Eddo-Lodge highlights this in her book *Why*

I'm No Longer Talking to White People About Race.[19] She highlights the need for white people to recognise their privilege and begin to acknowledge and discuss their complacency and passive participation within the system. As a collective staff body, and with our students, we must explore the assumptions we make and look at what the data and evidence is telling us.

Policies

Schools have always been fantastic at writing policies, but how often do we actually look at them and use them? It might happen when they are due for an update but some, particularly equality and diversity policies, should be discussed with staff on a regular basis. A familiar issue arises here too: how can we write, or even discuss, equality and diversity policies if we don't hear the voices of those we are trying to include and support? We can't develop such policies in isolation. It is essential to work closely with students and the wider school community. Consulting with representatives from different community groups should certainly be considered if they are not adequately represented in your own school.

Student, staff and community voice and development

Everything we have explored so far concerning the topic of voice comes back to actively listening to others' points of view. Schools must provide appropriate forums for discussion and agreed recommendations that come from these discussions must be actioned. It is not good enough to simply wait for something to go wrong and then respond reactively.

Does your school have safe havens at breaktime and lunchtime for students to meet and support those who are feeling isolated or picked on? Are there mentors on hand who can support these students? I have seen some amazing examples of this happening in schools, especially (but not exclusively) in sixth forms.

Regular staff training sessions are important, but we must do more than simply tick a box at the end of a training session and go off feeling content. Any training

---

19 Reni Eddo-Lodge, *Why I'm No Longer Talking to White People About Race* (London: Bloomsbury, 2017).

should have follow-up actions, perhaps in the form of action research where you can explore the training session in more depth.

Schools generally do a good job of celebrating cultural diversity through a wide variety of events, such as themed cookery evenings for students and parents, student fashion shows, language taster sessions, storytelling and school performances. When it works well, it filters down into lessons and teachers actively look for opportunities to bring out the richness of other cultures.

What to take from this chapter

We are moving towards a world where knowledge and information is readily available and schools are becoming less vital in the eyes of many students and parents. Schools can provide a hub that brings people together, face to face, in an environment where young people:

- Feel secure and safe.

- Learn to make sense of a world which is constantly changing.

- Are listened to.

- Have a say in how the school organises itself to respond to their needs.

- Take an active and accountable role in their own learning.

- Achieve their full potential.

- Are supported to develop good habits which they will take with them into adult life.

- Are encouraged to try out new ideas and take risks.

- Receive and reflect with others on their progress and development.

- Collaborate and contribute to their learning and the learning of others.

- Develop high aspirations, self-esteem and confidence in an atmosphere of unconditional respect.

- Have a base camp for life from which to soar!

To achieve this and to continue to attract students from our country's diverse range of cultures and backgrounds, we must create an ethos of genuine engagement and empowerment for the learner and a more responsive and relevant student-centred approach.

If you work in a school or are a stakeholder in a school – whether as a member of staff, parent, community group, local business or, most importantly, student – consider the questions below and begin to discuss these within or with your school:

● In what ways does your school embrace – within its curriculum, ethos and practices – the world within which your students live?

● What role (realistically) do students in your school have in making strategic decisions with regard to the vision, direction and running of the school?

● To what extent does your school allow students to choose the ways in which they learn (i.e. where, when, what and how quickly)?

● Has your school explored the reasons why there may be restrictions on the freedoms a student can be given (for example, how they learn)?

● To what extent does your school believe that it and other schools are the prime (if not the only) environments within which students can be educated in preparation for their adult and working lives?

● What barriers, if any, does the way your school organises its timetable or timings of the day work against developing ownership of learning?

● What would unconditional respect for students look like in your school?

● How does your school building and site encourage students to develop a sense of belonging (e.g. comfort, familiarity, safety and security, ownership)?

● To what extent do you feel that you are working in partnership with your school?

● How well does your school interact with the local community?

● How would you like to see your school interacting and working in partnership with the local community?

It is vital that we all play a part in the future development of schools in our communities. The first step is to create a sense of belonging, but in order to do so we need to respect and work with who and what young people are and the environment and world in which they live. We also need a deep knowledge and understanding of what stage our students are at in terms their physical, mental and emotional development. In addition, we must understand the temptations, distractions and pressures that society will throw at them today and in the future. Only if we can assimilate all this, can we work with young people to facilitate their development and send them on their journey towards fully formed adulthood.

Final Thoughts

When I first set out to write a book, it was in response to people asking me what I had done to turn around Eastern High. After starting to write, I soon realised that a book diarising my journey at the school might make for an entertaining read (if I had the skills to write it), but it would contribute little to helping school leaders develop the caring and insightful leadership necessary to create a positive school ethos. I also realised how much I detest the expression 'turn around a school'! It suggests that the job is over once you have rejuvenated the fortunes of a school. Too many head teachers have ridden on the crest of this wave, quickly gone on to bigger and better things and left a fragile school in their wake. Schools, especially those in deprived areas, require constant tending, nurturing and, at times, radical change.

In my opinion, the four areas described in this book – vision, leadership, positive relationships and belonging – are the greatest contributors to school ethos and, subsequently, to transforming the fortunes of a school. We tend to measure the success of schools using exam results, the percentage of good or better teaching, attendance and low exclusion rates. These are all outcomes of a sound school ethos. Unfortunately, some of them can be achieved through unsustainable means which are not necessarily in the best interests of the students. For example, exam outcomes can be inflated by placing students on courses that we know offer easy wins, or by intensive coaching in English and maths that is directed at those who will benefit whole-school outcomes the most or, most perniciously, by off-rolling. Similarly, attendance rates can be raised by ruthlessly following up non-attendance and fining parents. This is not the fault of the schools. We are all slaves to accountability measures which can so easily detract us from developing sustainable and effective practices.

It takes time for schools that have seen a downturn in their performance to rebuild robust systems and a strong ethos. Department areas don't take quite as long but neither can they transform overnight. As I near the end of my career as a head, I look back and think about the times I have tried to find a quick fix. This often came down to a lack of confidence when predicting how long sustainable transformation would take, together with the ceaseless pressure to be seen to be successful against performance measures in as short a time as possible.

However, self-confidence and the wherewithal to do what is right for the school doesn't have to come late in your career, and I hope this book has helped to provide some guidance towards developing schools with solid foundations and a clear direction.

I would like to leave you with three short lists: the first catalogues the main aspects of school improvement that have worked for me, the second highlights the tensions you will face and have to resolve as a school leader, and the third looks at what I might have done if I was given another opportunity.

Twelve considerations we should take into account when attempting to develop a transformational and sustainable school ethos

1 Always consider what is in the best interests of the student first.

2 You need to know yourself well to do this effectively. What do you value and believe in when it comes to education? What principles do you adhere to? How does this sit with what is in the best interests of the child? Test everything you introduce against your school's agreed principles, values and beliefs.

3 Spend time developing the school's vision and exploring its underlying values. They serve as the driver and unifying force.

4 Understand that the other stakeholders who are holding you to account may have agendas (likely political) which will be different to your own, so be prepared to rationalise your timescales. Accept that it will take time to bring about a transformation. Your job is to satisfy any interested parties that the outcomes will be sustainable and, in the meantime, the quality of learning will steadily improve for young people.

5 Be systematic. Have a prioritised plan and don't deviate from it unless it will improve your final outcomes.

6 However, accept that at times you will have to take the longer path to realise your ambitions. You will have to be pragmatic and compromise if you are

going to keep everyone on board along the way, but keep in mind your principles and values.

7   Model the behaviours you want to see and encourage your colleagues to do the same.

8   Encourage staff to make and maintain good relationships with their students and ensure you follow the same principles with those you lead and stakeholders with whom you work. If any of these relationships show signs of breaking down, you will need to know how to manage this back towards being a positive working relationship. Should the relationship flounder completely and looks unlikely to be repaired any time soon, you will need to move things on positively in the interim and, ultimately, find a way to restore it.

9   Keep things transparent. There should be no sudden surprises for staff or students. Provide opportunities for staff and student voice and involve them fully in any consultations. When you are unhappy with performance, let the person or department know. Don't leave them to second-guess your thoughts or go off with the false impression that things are fine, only to be told later they aren't – perhaps when it is too late.

10 Encourage professionalism. Teachers are regarded as professionals because they can be trusted to behave according to the written and unwritten codes of the profession. Don't let your colleagues forget this.

11 None of this is easy. You can work smartly to reduce the impact on your home life, but it is hard work, plain and simple. Get it right and you will shed a grateful tear every time an inspection goes your way, when you watch students open their exam results or when a parent or student thanks you out of the blue.

12 Never give up. I haven't managed to adhere to all of the above points all of the time. When my back has been up against the wall, I have wanted to escape and never return. At times like this, it has always been about finding that last bit of reserve deep inside and using it to lift myself back up, accompanied by the thought that there is a solution to every problem and a way to get things back on track. Do this and you will become stronger each time it happens.

Five tensions you will face and have to resolve

1   Sole decision-maker versus team player. If a whole-school matter requires a decision, when do you stop consulting with others and make it? Sometimes you will think you know the answer and your ego will push you to decide without consulting others. Sometimes you will ask for answers and feel reluctant to come to a conclusion. At some point you will have to be decisive, but never forget that you have a team around you to help.

2   Transparency versus withholding information. Transparency is essential if you want to keep your staff on board and feeling part of a team. However, sometimes too much information can cause needless anxiety and stress, especially when the whole picture is not yet clear. Being honest should always be the intention but finding the right time to be candid requires careful thought and consideration.

3   Stakeholder values versus your own values. At times, you and your team will be at odds with governors, local authorities and even parents. When this happens, explore what is in the best interest of the students. You may find that you need to re-evaluate your own values or articulate them more strongly and with evidence to back them up.

4   The benefits of sending staff on external courses (resulting in a well-trained workforce) versus lessons covered by supply staff. You will need to consider the possibility of creating your own bespoke training for staff and whether or not you have the capacity and expertise to do this. If staff do attend external courses, look for ways to enable them to share the learning with their colleagues. Keep a record of who is going off-site for meetings or training during the day, how often and for how long. This will help you to measure the benefits to the whole school versus the benefits to the individual.

5   Rules versus freedom. This can make or break a school ethos. Young people need boundaries, but they also need the opportunity to learn how to behave appropriately in various scenarios and without constant reminders in the form of posters and prompts. These can so easily build tension in a school which might be needless.

Eight things I would do differently if given another chance

1 Always be clear with individuals when I am not happy with something related to their work. It is better to do this straightaway and offer solutions, rather than allow the issue to build until it becomes too big to ignore and perhaps puts a person's job at risk.

2 Listen to my inner-self when everything inside me is screaming that the decision I am about to make is not the right one. (Don't forget the wealth of experience that helps to form intuition.)

3 Develop the strategy behind my vision before launching anything new or radical.

4 Delegate and then trust those to whom I have passed on responsibility. Monitoring processes can always be developed and implemented.

5 Involve the community far more in the school. Time spent on this is a good investment.

6 Work more with other schools and feeder primary schools. I have tried to do this, but there is always a tension when staff are out of school. I would like to think I have found the right balance but the time given over to collaboration never feels enough.

7 Accept that new ideas and initiatives take time to embed, not only in terms of systems and practices but also in people's minds. Be strategic concerning the frequency and quantity of new initiatives I launch and the impact this will have on the running of the school.

8 Remember that I have my own family to get home to, and so organise myself effectively to enable me to achieve a sensible work–life balance.

Bibliography

Adams, Richard (2019). 'Schools Pushing Children into Home Schooling Say Councils', *The Guardian* (17 January). Available at: https://www.theguardian.com/education/2019/jan/17/schools-pushing-children-into-home-schooling-say-councils.

Anderson, Jane (2016). 'The Teenage Brain Under Construction', *American College of Paediatricians* (May). Available at: https://acpeds.org/position-statements/the-teenage-brain-under-construction.

Belbin, Meredith R. (2010). *Management Teams: Why They Succeed or Fail*, 3rd edn. Abingdon and New York: Routledge.

Bulman, May (2019). 'Children "Falling Off the Grid" in the Tens of Thousands Amid Surge in Pupils Leaving Mainstream Education', *The Independent* (3 February). Available at: https://www.independent.co.uk/news/uk/home-news/home-schooling-education-children-commissioner-anne-longfield-a8760951.html.

Burnett, Jane (2018). 'Survey: 34% of Employers Reprimanded or Fired Someone Over Online Content', *The Ladders* (15 August). Available at: https://www.theladders.com/career-advice/survey-34-of-companies-reprimanded-or-fired-an-employee-over-online-content.

Cadwalladr, Carole (2015). 'The Granny Cloud: The Network of Volunteers Helping Poorer Children Learn', *The Guardian* (2 August). Available at: https://www.theguardian.com/education/2015/aug/02/sugata-mitra-school-in-the-cloud.

Cherry, Kendra (2017). 'What Is Attachment Theory? The Importance of Early Emotional Bonds', *VeryWellMind* (17 July). Available at: https://www.verywellmind.com/what-is-attachment-theory-2795337.

Cherry, Kendra (2020). 'Characteristics of Ego Strength', *Very Well Mind* (30 April). Available at: https://www.verywellmind.com/ego-strength-2795169.

Chiong, Charleen, Menzies, Loic and Parameshwaran, Meenakshi (2017). 'Why Do Long-Serving Teachers Stay in the Teaching Profession? Analysing the Motivations of Teachers with 10 or More Years' Experience in England', *British Educational Research Journal* 43(6): 1083–1110.

Claxton, Guy (2002). *Building Learning Power: Helping People to Become Better Learners*. Bristol: TLO.

Corrigan, John (2019). *Red Brain Blue Brain: Living, Loving and Leading without Fear*. Leichhardt, NSW: Castleflag.

Covey, Stephen R. (1989). *The 7 Habits of Highly Effective People: Powerful Lessons in Personal Change*. New York: Free Press.

Crown Prosecution Service (2019). 'Restorative Justice' (24 September). Available at: https://www.cps.gov.uk/legal-guidance/restorative-justice.

Day, Christopher and Sammons, Pamela (2014). *Successful School Leadership*. Reading: Education Development Trust. Available at: https://www.educationdevelopmenttrust.com/EducationDevelopmentTrust/files/a3/a359e571-7033-41c7-8fe7-9ba60730082e.pdf.

Department for Education (2019). *Relationships Education, Relationships and Sex Education (RSE) and Health Education: Statutory Guidance for Governing Bodies, Proprietors, Head Teachers, Principals, Senior Leadership Teams, Teachers* (updated July 2020). Available at: https://www.

gov.uk/government/publications/relationships-education-relationships-and-sex-education-rse-and-health-education.

Department for Education and Gibb, Nick (2015). 'The Purpose of Education' [transcript] (9 July). Available at: https://www.gov.uk/government/speeches/the-purpose-of-education.

Donaldson, Graham (2015). *Successful Futures: Independent Review of Curriculum and Assessment Arrangements in Wales* [Donaldson Review]. Available at: https://gov.wales/sites/default/files/publications/2018-03/successful-futures.pdf.

Dweck, Carol S. (2007). *Mindset: The New Psychology of Success*. New York: Ballantine Books.

Eddo-Lodge, Reni (2017). *Why I'm No Longer Talking to White People About Race*. London: Bloomsbury.

Education Endowment Foundation (2018). *The Attainment Gap 2017*. Available at: https://educationendowmentfoundation.org.uk/public/files/Annual_Reports/EEF_Attainment_Gap_Report_2018.pdf.

Education Scotland (2015). *How Good Is Our School?*, 4th edn. Available at: https://education.gov.scot/improvement/Documents/Frameworks_SelfEvaluation/FRWK2_NIHeditHGIOS/FRWK2_HGIOS4.pdf.

Education and Training Inspectorate (2017). *Effective Practice and Self-Evaluation Questions for Post-Primary*. Available at: https://www.etini.gov.uk/sites/etini.gov.uk/files/publications/isef-post-primary-with-shared-ed.pdf.

Estyn (2020). *The Annual Report of Her Majesty's Chief Inspector of Education and Training in Wales 2018–2019*. Available at: https://www.estyn.gov.wales/sites/www.estyn.gov.wales/files/2020-07/Annual_Report_2018_2019_en_2.pdf.

Foster, David and Danechi, Shadi (2019). *Home Education in England*. House of Commons Library Briefing Paper No. 5108. Available at: https://commonslibrary.parliament.uk/research-briefings/sn05108.

Freud, Sigmund (1961 [1923]). 'The Ego and the Id', in *The Standard Edition of the Complete Psychological Works of Sigmund Freud, Volume XIX (1923–1925): The Ego and the Id and Other Works*. London: Hogarth Press, pp. 1–66.

Fullan, Michael, Bennett, Barrie and Rolheiser-Bennett, Carol (1990). 'Linking Classroom and School Improvement', *Educational Leadership* (May): 13–19. Available at: http://www.ascd.org/ASCD/pdf/journals/ed_lead/el_199005_fullan.pdf.

Gallo, Carmine (2012). 'Richard Branson: "If It Can't Fit on the Back of an Envelope, It's Rubbish" (an Interview)', *Forbes* (22 October). Available at: https://www.forbes.com/sites/carminegallo/2012/10/22/richard-branson-if-it-cant-fit-on-the-back-of-an-envelope-its-rubbish-interview/?sh=409934b31ae9.

Gallo, Carmine (2018). 'Jeff Bezos Banned PowerPoint in Meetings. His Replacement is Brilliant', *Inc.* (25 April). Available at: https://www.inc.com/carmine-gallo/jeff-bezos-bans-powerpoint-in-meetings-his-replacement-is-brilliant.html.

Galvan, Adriana (2010). 'Adolescent Development of the Reward System', *Frontiers in Human Neuroscience* 4(6). Available at: https://www.ncbi.nlm.nih.gov/pmc/articles/PMC2826184.

Gladwell, Malcolm (2005). *Blink: The Power of Thinking without Thinking*. London: Penguin.

Guilbault, Lauren (2021). 'What's the Best Way to Define Ego?', *BetterHelp* (7 May). Available at: https://www.betterhelp.com/advice/willpower/whats-the-best-way-to-define-ego.

Gunnell, David, Kidger, Judi and Elvidge, Hamish (2018). 'Adolescent Mental Health in Crisis', *BMJ* 361: k2608. DOI:10.1136/bmj.k2608

Hall, Karyn (2014). 'Create a Sense of Belonging', *Psychology Today* (24 March). Available at: https://www.psychologytoday.com/gb/blog/pieces-mind/201403/create-sense-belonging.

Harari, Yuval N. (2014). *Sapiens: A Brief History of Humankind*. London: Harvill Secker.

Harris, Michael (2015). *The End of Absence: Reclaiming What We've Lost in a World of Constant Connection*. New York: Penguin.

Hattenstone, Alix and Lawrie, Eleanor (2021). 'Covid: Home-Education Numbers Rise by 75%', *BBC News* (19 July). Available at: https://www.bbc.co.uk/news/education-57255380.

Hattie, John (2011). *Visible Learning for Teachers: Maximizing Impact on Learning*. Abingdon and New York: Routledge.

Hook, Sidney (1963). *Education for Modern Man: A New Perspective*. New York: Alfred A. Knopf.

Hughes, Thomas (1857). *Tom Brown's School Days*. London: Macmillan.

Klein, Melanie (1997 [1959]). 'Our Adult World and its Roots in Infancy', in *Envy and Gratitude and Other Works 1946–1963*. London: Vintage, pp. 247–263.

Leadsom, Andrea, Field, Frank, Burstow, Paul and Lucas, Caroline (2013). *The 1001 Critical Days: The Importance of the Conception to Age Two Period. A Cross-Party Manifesto*. Available at: https://www.nwcscnsenate.nhs.uk/files/8614/7325/1138/1001cdmanifesto.pdf.

McClees Jr, Ernest L. (2016). 'School Mission Statements: A Look at Influencing Behaviour', *International Journal of Humanities and Social Science Review* 2(1): 50–54. Available at: http://www.ijhssrnet.com/uploads/volumes/1598808998.pdf.

McLeod, Saul (2019). 'Id, Ego and Superego', *Simply Psychology* (25 September). Available at: https://www.simplypsychology.org/psyche.html.

Mitra, Sugata (2013). 'Build a School in the Cloud' [video], *TED.com* (February). Available at: https://www.ted.com/talks/sugata_mitra_build_a_school_in_the_cloud?language=en.

Mosley, Jenny (2013). *Quality Circle Time in the Secondary School: A Handbook of Good Practice*, 2nd edn. Abingdon and New York: Routledge.

Mowat, Andrew, Corrigan, John and Long, Doug (2009). *The Success Zone: 5 Powerful Steps to Growing Yourself and Leading Others*. Mount Evelyn, VIC: Global Publishing.

Ofcom (2019). 'Why Children Spend Time Online' (4 February). Available at: https://www.ofcom.org.uk/about-ofcom/latest/features-and-news/why-children-spend-time-online.

Office for National Statistics (2020). 'Young People Not in Education, Employment or Training (NEET), UK: August 2020'. Available at: https://www.ons.gov.uk/employmentandlabourmarket/peoplenotinwork/unemployment/bulletins/youngpeoplenotineducationemploymentortrainingneet/august2020.

Ofsted (2021). *Education Inspection Framework* (updated 23 July). Available at: https://www.gov.uk/government/publications/education-inspection-framework/education-inspection-framework.

Pearlman, Bob (2004). 'Elements of Transformation: Transforming Secondary Schools for the 21st Century' [PowerPoint] (12 November). Available at: http://www.bobpearlman.org/Kent.htm.

Ray, Brian D. (2020). 'Homeschooling: The Research', *National Home Education Research Institute* (3 May). Available at: https://www.nheri.org/research-facts-on-homeschooling.

Rejholic, Tod (2002). 'An Action Research on the Effects of Extrinsic Rewards on Motivation of Eighth Grade Language Arts Students'. Available at: https://files.eric.ed.gov/fulltext/ED473051.pdf.

Robbins, Mel (2017). *The 5 Second Rule: The Fastest Way to Change Your Life*. New York: Savio Republic.

Robinson, Ken (2010). 'RSA Animate: Changing Education Paradigms' [video] (14 October). Available at: https://www.youtube.com/watch?v=zDZFcDGpL4U&t=144s.

Robinson, Viviane, Hohepa, Margie and Lloyd, Claire (2009). *School Leadership and Student Outcomes: Identifying What Works and Why. Best Evidence Syntheses Iteration (BES)*. New Zealand: Ministry of Education. Available at: https://www.educationcounts.govt.nz/__data/assets/pdf_file/0015/60180/BES-Leadership-Web-updated-foreword-2015.pdf.

Salem, Richard (2003). 'Empathic Listening', *Beyond Intractability* (July). Available at: https://www.beyondintractability.org/essay/empathic_listening.

Sawyer, Susan M., Azzopardi, Peter S., Wickremarathne, Dakshitha and Patton, George C. (2018). 'The Age of Adolescence', *Lancet Child Adolescent Health* 2(3): 223–228. DOI:10.1016/S2352-4642(18)30022-1

Scarpino, Philip V. (2009). 'Reverend Theodore Hesburgh Oral History Interview', *Tobias Leadership Center* (6 January). Available at: https://tobiascenter.iu.edu/research/oral-history/audio-transcripts/hesburgh-theodore.html.

Schieber, Philip (1987). 'The Wit and Wisdom of Grace Hopper', *OCLC Newsletter*, 167 (March/April). Available at: http://www.cs.yale.edu/homes/tap/Files/hopper-wit.html.

Schonert-Reichl, Kimberly (2000). 'Children and Youth at Risk: Some Conceptual Considerations'. Paper prepared for the Pan-Canadian Education Research Agenda Symposium, Ottawa, 6–7 April. Available at: https://www.researchgate.net/profile/Kimberly-Schonert-Reichl/publication/237308266_Children_and_Youth_at_Risk_Some_Conceptual_Considerations/links/00b7d526f0df311b49000000/Children-and-Youth-at-Risk-Some-Conceptual-Considerations.pdf.

Seladi-Schulman, Jill (2018). 'What Part of the Brain Controls Emotions?', *Healthline* (23 July). Available at: www.healthline.com/health/what-part-of-the-brain-controls-emotions.

Shatzer, Ryan H. (2009). 'A Comparison Study Between Instructional and Transformational Leadership Theories: Effects on Student Achievement and Teacher Job Satisfaction'. Dissertation, Brigham Young University. Available at: https://scholarsarchive.byu.edu/etd/2432.

Sinek, Simon (2009). *Start with Why: How Great Leaders Inspire Everyone to Take Action*. New York: Penguin.

Smith, Matthew (2017). 'Disgracebook: One in Five Employers Have Turned Down a Candidate Because of Social Media', *YouGov* (10 April). Available at: https://yougov.co.uk/topics/politics/articles-reports/2017/04/10/disgracebook-one-five-employers-have-turned-down-c.

Spear, Linda P. (2013). 'Adolescent Neurodevelopment', *Journal of Adolescent Health* 52(2, Supp. 2): S7–13. DOI:10.1016/j.jadohealth.2012.05.006

Wargo, Eric (2006). 'How Many Seconds to a First Impression?', *Association for Psychological Science* (1 July). Available at: https://www.psychologicalscience.org/observer/how-many-seconds-to-a-first-impression.

Warnock, Mary (1978). *Report of the Committee of Enquiry into the Education of Handicapped Children and Young People* [Warnock Report]. London: HMSO. Available at: http://www.educationengland.org.uk/documents/warnock.

Whittaker, Freddie (2020). 'Investigation: Minister Intervenes As Home Education Soars', *Schools Week* (23 October). Available at: https://schoolsweek.co.uk/investigation-minister-intervenes-as-home-education-soars.

Woodham, Chai (2015). 'Why Kids Are Hitting Puberty Earlier Than Ever', *US News* (17 April). Available at: https://health.usnews.com/health-news/health-wellness/articles/2015/04/17/why-kids-are-hitting-puberty-earlier-than-ever.